PRAYERS FOR THE LORD'S DAY

PRAYERS FOR THE LORD'S DAY

Hope for the Exiles

James S. Lowry

Geneva Press
Louisville, Kentucky

Scripture quotations, unless otherwise indicated, are from the New Revised Standard Version of the Bible, copyright © 1989 by the Division of Christian Education of the National Council of the Churches of Christ in the U.S.A. and are used by permission.

Excerpt from *Cadences of Home: Preaching among Exiles* by Walter Brueggemann. © 1997 Walter Brueggemann. Used by permission of Westminster John Knox Press.

Book design by Sharon Adams
Cover design by Pam Poll Graphic Design
Cover photography by Greg Schneider

First edition
Published by Geneva Press
Louisville, Kentucky

This book is printed on acid-free paper that meets the American National Standards Institute Z39.48 standard. ∞

PRINTED IN THE UNITED STATES OF AMERICA

02 03 04 05 06 07 08 09 10 11 — 10 9 8 7 6 5 4 3 2 1

Library of Congress Cataloging-in-Publication Data

Lowry, James S.
    Prayers for the Lord's day : hope for the exiles / James S. Lowry
      p. cm.
    ISBN 0-664-50229-6 (alk. paper)
    1. Pastoral prayers. I. Title.

  BV250 .L69 2002
  264'.13—dc21   2002022782

Contents

Acknowledgments

I once overheard a brilliant scholar struggling to recall the source of an insight he was sharing with an informal gathering of admirers. Try as he might, he could recall neither title nor author. Finally, in desperation, the scholar shrugged and said, "Oh, well, everything I know I learned from someone else."

He was wrong, of course; or at least he was not altogether right. I know him well and know him to have had far more than his share of original thoughts. Still, there are long and graceful shadows of truth in his casual remark. In all events, my scholarly friend set me to being grateful for everything I know that owes its genesis to someone else.

There is one sense in which the prayers in this little volume are all mine. I wrote every one of them. There is a far more important sense, however, in which none of these prayers is mine. They are the prayers of a swarm of faithful teachers, most of whom had no clue they were teaching me to pray. More than that, they were teaching me to engage bravely the dangerous business of forming prayers for others.

My parents, Bright and Rebecca Lowry, long since gone to pray with the hosts of heaven, are at the head of the list. The reverent candor with which they spoke to God following breakfast every (every!) morning of my childhood and youth set me early on the path to recognize that the earnest prayer of one, carefully and thoughtfully formed, could be the prayer of all at the table. I am grateful. The brave and faithful congregations of God's people who called me to be preacher and pastor for them have kept me carefully in the path of forming prayers for others. I readily confess, however, that unlike the prayers that flowed so freely from my father and mother at the breakfast table, fashioning prayer for groups of God's people has never come naturally for me. In fact, the burden or responsibility for such praying weighs heavily. It always has. Even now, after nearly four decades of leading public worship regularly, I do not like to be called on to pray extemporaneously on behalf of others. I am, therefore, deeply obliged to the faithful who assembled often to worship and insisted that I give words to their prayers. Unwittingly, they kept me disciplined in the art of writing prayers. The congregations I have served as installed pastor are The Church of the Good Shepherd (Presbyterian) in Anniston, Alabama; First Presbyterian Church of Marianna, Florida; Orange Park Presbyterian Church near Jacksonville, Florida; Mount Pleasant Presbyterian Church near Charleston, South Carolina; and Idlewild Presbyterian Church in Memphis, Tennessee. Many fine teachers taught me the theology of prayer, but none taught me more about praying than those faithful communities of worship and mission. I am grateful.

Two additional congregations have honored me by calling me to be their interim pastor. They are the First Presbyterian Church of New Bern, North Carolina, and Government Street Presbyterian Church in Mobile, Alabama. They have not only let me form prayers for them in worship but have afforded me time to write books, including this one. I am grateful.

In ways quite practical, I am grateful to Pat Taylor for her faithful and capable copyediting. She can spot a comma splice from across the room. That's the least of it. She has made countless corrections to the manuscript of this book, without once doing damage to this writer's ego. I am grateful.

Martha Nichols Lowry has been my marriage partner for nearly forty years. She is yet remarkably full of love and grace and surprises and encouragement all tempered with patience and impatience in exactly the right balance. I am particularly grateful for her good-natured willingness to pull up stakes and move often during this time in my career when I am combining interim pastorates and writing.

Finally, I am grateful to daughters Jayne Stallworth Lowry and Anne Nichols Lowry, who were subjects of my prayers for long months before they were born and especially on the two October nights, separated by three years and a handful of days, when they each, in turn, brought their own brands of unspeakable joy into our lives. They are answers to prayers of thanks so deep they can only be expressed in deep sighs of satisfaction. To them these pages are dedicated along with my pledge to them to keep on praying.

Introduction

My hard assumption here in the first full year of the twenty-first century is that the last tattered shreds of the Christian church's imperial domination and influence are forever faded, Christendom has fallen from power, and all Christians are living and worshiping in what may helpfully be known as exile. This book is a collection of prayers intended as a resource for pastors and others who regularly lead Christian exiles in worship.

Coming to terms with the loss of imperial power and influence has not been easy for the church. Articulating the reality of the loss was the first and crucially important step. In that regard, a handful of scholars has been enormously influential. Stanley Hauerwas and William H. Willimon come immediately to mind. While I disagree with some of their conclusions, their book *Resident Aliens: Life in the Christian Colony* (Abingdon, 1989) has become a landmark for those who seek to understand the church in contemporary culture. As the title of their book says clearly, Hauerwas and Willimon see Christians living as aliens in a culture foreign to the way of Christianity. Others, notably Walter Brueggemann, make a similar and I believe more helpful observation using the Old Testament image of exile as metaphor for latter-day Christianity. That is, while Brueggemann and others recognize that contemporary Christian exile is not geographic as was the case for Jews in the Old Testament, they nevertheless see many other similarities between the ancient Jewish exile and what they name contemporary Christian exile.

The first and most easily identified similarity between latter-day Christianity and ancient Jews exiled in Egypt and centuries later in Babylon is that an increasingly secular world is simply enveloping and overpowering Christianity to the extent that Christianity is no longer an influence of any identifiable socioeconomic significance. For the faithful, however, Brueggemann sees a much more important and far more compelling similarity. For him,

Christian exile is not simply a passive acquiescence to the powers that be. He sees faithful Christians in exile as living over against those powers:

> [Since] serious, reflective Christians find themselves increasingly at odds with the dominant values of consumer capitalism and its support-ive military patriotism . . . there is no easy or obvious way to hold together core faith claims and the social realities around us. . . . If it be insisted that the church members are still in places of social power and influence, I suggest that Christians only need to act and speak out of any serious conviction concerning the public claims of the gospel, and it becomes promptly evident that we are outsiders to the flow of power.[1]

As a pastor/preacher who is regularly privileged to lead "serious reflective Christians" in worship, I find the image of Christian exile extremely helpful and strangely hopeful. On the one hand, by using the metaphor of exile for our loss of power and influence, our loss can be confessed and lamented. Such confession and lament is necessary whether our power and influence were pil-fered by forces outside the camp, squandered by foolishness inside the camp, abandoned as something we should never have had, or taken from us by Holy God who, at last, will not tolerate our groveling after "the gods of the people in whose land you now dwell."[2]

On the other hand, by using the image of Christian exile, Christians can be filled with hope that does not rest on imperial power but on the power of a gracious God who has a long history of restoring exiles to God's own promise. In the end, as a matter of our sure belief, the promise of God will not at last be thwarted. Moreover, we dare also to believe the Christian movement, freed from the bonds of Christendom, is being given a fresh opportunity to play a missional role in the unfolding of God's promise for all of God's people. In this new missional role, we continue to stand before God on behalf of all peo-ple and proclaim boldly the truth of God known to us in Jesus Christ. At the same time, we humbly confess that the saving God whom we worship is not bound by our movement, as has been, until lately, claimed by Christendom.

Because that is so, contemporary Christian exiles have much to learn from our Jewish forebears from whom we are bold to claim such a strong metaphor. A survey of the canonical literature from and/or about the exile period is both disturbing and hopeful. Consider what must surely be Ezekiel's most famous vision of Israel in Babylonian exile:

> The hand of the LORD came upon me, and he brought me out by the spirit of the LORD and set me down in the middle of a valley; it was full of bones. He led me all around them; there were very many lying in the val-

ley, and they were very dry. He said to me, "Mortal, can these bones live?" (Ezek. 37:1–3a)

Later the prophet says:

> So I prophesied as I had been commanded; and as I prophesied, suddenly there was a noise, a rattling, and the bones came together, bone to its bone. I looked, and there were sinews on them, and flesh had come upon them, and skin had covered them; but there was no breath in them. Then he said to me, "Prophesy to the breath, prophesy, mortal, and say to the breath: Thus says the Lord GOD: Come from the four winds, O breath, and breathe upon these slain, that they may live." I prophesied as he commanded me, and the breath came into them, and they lived, and stood on their feet, a vast multitude. (37:7–10)

Nothing could be more disturbing than to envision the contemporary church after the death of Christendom as Ezekiel envisioned ancient Israel in captivity. A valley strewn with dry bones is not a pretty image. Yet, when in our powerlessness we can find little to do but engage in endless internecine bickering among ourselves, the image is frighteningly up-to-date and accurate. On the other hand, nothing could be more hopeful than to envision the church, as Ezekiel envisioned ancient Israel, with the breath of God breathing new life into God's own covenant people. The effort of this book of prayers is not, in most instances, to replicate biblical images. Rather, this is an attempt, however faltering, to learn from the power of biblical language and replicate that power in developing useful images that, on the one hand, reflect our Christian exilic reality and, on the other hand, express the promise of our hope as Christian people.

Isaiah is another case in point. Setting aside for the moment important questions of date and authorship and using the prophecy as a canonical unit, consider side-by-side the following passages from what are commonly called First Isaiah and Third Isaiah, respectively. Each is an expression of successive reality for ancient Israel. The first is from before the exile when exile was looming on the near horizon, and the second is from near the end of the exile. The first deals realistically with danger. The second deals realistically with a vision of hope-filled mission:

> Hear, O heavens, and listen, O earth;
>   for the LORD has spoken:
> I reared children and brought them up,
>   but they have rebelled against me.
> The ox knows its owner,
>   and the donkey its master's crib;

> but Israel does not know,
>> my people do not understand.
>>> (Isa. 1:2–3)

Later comes a text that expresses Israel's mission. As it happened, it was the very text to which Jesus claimed to be the fulfillment:

> The spirit of the Lord GOD is upon me,
>> because the LORD has anointed me;
> he has sent me to bring good news to the oppressed,
>> to bind up the brokenhearted,
> to proclaim liberty to the captives,
>> and release to the prisoners;
> to proclaim the year of the LORD's favor,
>> and the day of vengeance of our God;
>> to comfort all who mourn.
>
> . . . .
> They shall build up the ancient ruins,
>> they shall raise up the former devastations;
> they shall repair the ruined cities,
>> the devastations of many generations.
>>> (61:1–2, 4)[3]

Again, from these and countless other passages like them taken from the exilic experience of ancient Israel, I have learned the importance of vivid language in expressing the longing and hope of the church.

The Psalter, of course, is rich with similar but more closely paired examples of intense expressions of honesty in desperation and honesty in hope that come from the anguish and comfort of exile and deliverance remembered. The haunting refrain recalling the enduring steadfast love of God makes Psalm 136 a magnificent case in point, as the poet recalls the exile and deliverance of God's own people. After giving thanks to God and naming God God of gods and Lord of lords, the poet sets out on a captivating litany that draws the worshipers from the memory of the wonder of creation to the memory of the horror of exile to the memory of deliverance, all set in the context of God's enduring love:

> [God] who by understanding made the heavens,
>> for his steadfast love endures forever;
> who spread out the earth on the waters,
>> for his steadfast love endures forever;
>
> . . . .

[who] brought Israel out from among [the Egyptians]
    for his steadfast love endures forever;
. . . .
who divided the Red Sea in two,
    for his steadfast love endures forever.
                     (Ps. 136:5–6, 11, 13)

The poet concludes:

It is he who remembered us in our low estate,
    for his steadfast love endures forever;
and rescued us from our foes,
    for his steadfast love endures forever;
who gives food to all flesh,
    for his steadfast love endures forever.
O give thanks to the God of heaven,
    for his steadfast love endures forever.
                     (Ps. 136:23–26)

As in the examples from Isaiah and the Psalter, the prayers in this volume attempt to expose before God the hope of exiled Christianity by acknowledging before God our experience of contrasting the false hope of imperial mission with the hopeful mission of God as given to exiled Christians.

Apocalyptic literature drawn from Hebrew exile provides yet another set of examples where the use of language and image expressed the hope of exiles. Consider the well-known account from the book of Daniel where the powerful captor king, Belshazzer, son of the mighty Nebuchadnezzar, sees a vision of a hand writing on the wall and only the exiled Daniel can interpret the vision. When Daniel is given vast imperial power as a reward for his insight, he refuses to adopt the way of imperial power. For refusing to worship the emperor, Daniel is summarily thrown into the lions' den, where, as every child who has ever been to Sunday school must surely remember, Daniel is protected from all harm by the God who protects faithful exiles. Once again, learning from those and other images like them, I have attempted to form prayers which use language and images from our culture that recognize the important and dangerous interpretive role of exiles in our culture. The prayers, then, anticipate that God will fulfill God's promise of deliverance with graphic faithfulness.

Since in my view all Christians are in exile, by deduction, one could logically conclude these prayers are intended for all Christians. Nevertheless, I readily admit there are some groups of exiled Christians for whom I hope (and pray!) these prayers will be particularly appealing and expressive. For example, I would like nothing better than for those Christian exiles who have refused to retreat into hiding to watch for the church to join Christendom in death to find these prayers curiously hopeful. In much the same way, in these prayers I have tried to find language that will be useful to those exiled Christians who recognize that the Christendom of either liberal or conservative mainline Protestantism can never be and should never be resurrected. Moreover, I hope the language of these prayers will be helpful to those Christians who while in exile are able to recognize and value the absolute necessity of diversity in our ranks. Likewise, I pray that those Christians who refuse to free themselves from exile by joining the captors and living either at the fringe of the community of faith or moving outside the camp altogether will be able to take comfort in these prayers.

In short, these prayers are intended as a liturgical resource especially for those Christians who have come to believe to the marrow of their bone, as I have come to believe to the marrow of my bone, that despite all outward evidence to the contrary, the Christian church has in, around, and before it greater hope than it has had since before the fourth century when the emperor Constantine gave us the curse of imperial credibility. It is now abundantly clear that the Christian church has no one on whom to depend save God and the faithful people of God. Therein lies our hope. Those among us who use images from the business world to talk about the church of Jesus Christ are false prophets. They suggest bold new ventures for the church to thrive again by joining together in user-friendly, full-service groupings of people who look and act alike so each group can claim what they shamelessly call their "market share" of available believers. As alluring as their voices are, they should not be heeded by the deeply faithful. Likewise, those would-be prophets who use images from the Old West are not to be trusted. They suggest we "circle the wagons," take comfort in the safety of each other's company, and together fend off the world that is alien to our way of believing and doing. They are blind prophets, or at least they see, at best, only half the truth. We do well to take comfort in each other's company, but to "circle the wagons" and shut out the world is blasphemy against the God who calls us to go into the world.

In my view, only those prophets who are able to see that the Christian church has today unparalleled opportunities for faithfulness will be named the true prophets of the early years of our third millennium as followers of Christ. The prayers in this book are an effort to give language to their beseeching as they lead the exiles in worship. As Walter Brueggemann notes:

> [A] new circumstance [of exile] suggests a very different posture for preaching and pastoral authority. . . . Exile did not lead Jews in the Old Testament to abandon faith or to settle for abdicating despair, nor to retreat to private religion. On the contrary, exile evoked the most brilliant literature and most daring theological articulation in the Old Testament.[4]

This book, then, is a compilation of prayers written for worshiping congregations. Using the words of Walter Brueggemann, I make no claim that this little volume approaches being "brilliant literature." The prayers on these pages, however, come from the heart, the mind, the bone marrow, and the spleen of one disciplined in the art of worship in the Reformed tradition and who believes deeply that God yet calls the followers of Jesus to serious reflective worship and a mission of true hope in a world dominated by despair and the promise of false hopes.

Except as the prayers of confession and litanies contained here were published in various church worship bulletins, none was written for the purpose of being published. To the contrary, with but a few exceptions, each was written for public worship for a specific gathering of Christians on a specific day in a specific context for a specific reason or clutch of reasons. I was tempted to edit the prayers to make them more universally useful for busy pastors. Every effort to do that, however, failed miserably and left the prayers sterile and hollow. Except, therefore, for minor editing, the prayers presented here are exactly as they were used on a specific Lord's Day or other time exiles were gathered for worship. Where necessary, I note the context or circumstance in which a prayer was written. Other times, the prayers themselves will make the context obvious.

A special word of explanation must be added concerning the brief collection of prayers in chapter 5, "Prayers of Exiles Praying outside the Camp." These prayers are included for two reasons. First, in my view, we Christian exiles must recognize there are yet some pockets in our post-Christendom world where exiled Christians working in public places long for public prayer to be integral to the discharge of their duties. Some, of course, are simply diehards who refuse to face the reality of Christendom's death. Praying publicly at high school football games, for example, seems, at best, silly and, at worst, heretical. For others among the faithful, however, asking their pastor to pray at certain public events is both natural and crucially important to them. Their request must, if possible, be honored. Happily, telling the difference between the diehards and the faithful is not usually very difficult. Moreover, in addition to faithful individuals, there are yet some public events that cry out for public prayer. This book includes, for example, prayers from the balcony of the Loraine Motel—where Martin Luther King Jr. was assassinated—and at an NAACP gathering.

The second reason I have included the brief collection in chapter 5 is that, in my view, Christian exiles must be keenly aware that when we are praying outside the camp we can no longer assume our ecumenical partners include only sisters and brothers of other Christian denominations. It is my contention—in our praying as well as in our living—that we can honor other religious traditions without denying our own. The prayers in chapter 5 are an effort to illustrate how that can be done.

This book is a resource for pastors and other worship leaders, not primarily a trove of prayers from which to draw. To be sure, any of these prayers may be used verbatim or altered appropriately to fit a particular circumstance. As a matter of fact, I have on numerous occasions edited many of these prayers for use with more than one worshiping congregation. If, for example, a busy pastor is facing a bulletin deadline and needs a prayer of confession to give to the secretary before rushing off to conduct a funeral, or if a busy pastor wakes up on a given Lord's Day and discovers she has not had time to work on a pastoral prayer or needs some examples to provide a lay worship leader, using or adapting one or more of these prayers is appropriate. (The publisher explains on the copyright page of this book that these prayers may be published on a one-time basis in church bulletins without seeking permission. Geneva Press is, after all, in the business of providing resources for the church. I gladly make my modest contribution to its effort.)

Having said that, however, I hope that the language of these prayers might serve to encourage busy pastors and others who lead Christians in worship to take seriously the importance of their own honest and vivid prayers that express faithfully the reality and hope of the particular exiles with whom they live and worship.

The prayers are presented in five chapters. Only the first two (and largest), "Prayers of Confession for Exiles at Worship" and "Pastoral Prayers for Exiles at Worship on the Lord's Day," are ordered according to the liturgical year. In those chapters, the season for each prayer is noted. The prayers in the remaining chapters are presented in random order. Where necessary, however, the table of contents has extensive subheadings. The prayers are numbered sequentially for ease of reference.

Chapter 1

Prayers of Confession for Exiles at Worship

A Prayer of Confession for Advent (1)

Lord God, forgive us.
In the matter of peace
  we tend to trust
  what seems to us
  the more prudent promises:
    Balanced power;
    Unshakable earth;
    Solid dollar.
Give us this day
  ears to anticipate the angels singing
  of peace of a different birth.
We pray in the name of Jesus Christ. Amen.

A Prayer of Confession for Christmas Eve (2)

Lord God, forgive our clouded memory:
  In the dark crevices of our hiding
    we forget how you said,
      "Let there be light."
  In the confused turns of our choosing
    we forget how you said,
      "You shall have no other gods."
  In the lonely corners of our living
    we forget how you said,
      "To us a child is born."

Fulfill in this place tonight
    the truth you spoke long ago.
We pray in the name of Jesus Christ. Amen.

❦❦❦❦❦❦❦

A Prayer of Confession for the Sunday after Christmas (3)

Lord God, forgive our weary dreaming
    that gives up on the hope of seeing
        justice roll down like waters,
        a peaceable kingdom, and
        truth to set us free.
Lord God, forgive our tired singing
    that sets no rafters ringing:
        with peace on earth, goodwill to all,
        with the Lord God omnipotent reigneth, and
        with joy to the world.
Give us grace, O God,
    that these days of our lives
    be filled with vision and praise,
    through Jesus Christ our Lord. Amen.

❦❦❦❦❦❦❦

A Prayer of Confession for Lent or Ordinary Time (4)

Lord God,
    few of us misunderstand you all of the time,
    but all of us misunderstand you some of the time:
        Your thoughts on happiness;
        Your ideas on giving;
        Your way of making whole.
These are not always our ready choices.
Give us faith, we pray,
    to risk a dangerous hope,
    to be ready to think as you teach, and
    to act as you lead.
We pray in the name of Jesus Christ. Amen.

❦❦❦❦❦❦❦

A Prayer of Confession for Lent or Ordinary Time (5)

Lord God, forgive us.
   Unlike the psalmist,
      when we walk through the shadow of death,
      we sometimes fear evil.
   Unlike Paul,
      we are not always sure that nothing can separate us
      from the love of God in Christ Jesus our Lord.
   Unlike John of Patmos,
      in the midst of injustice
      we do not always see a new heaven and a new earth.
         Forgive again, we pray,
            our feeble use of the faith you give,
            and restore to us the hope of trust
            and the trust of hope.
         We pray in the name of Jesus Christ. Amen.

A Prayer of Confession for Lent or Ordinary Time (6)

Merciful God, forgive us.
   We live as though you have made no promises:
      Chasing after monotonous dreams,
         we busy ourselves with meager plans.
      Clinging to drab visions,
         we pursue paltry resolutions.
         Restore our souls, O God.
         Inspire within us such imagination
            that we may address with optimism
            the needs of this and every day.
         We pray in the name of Jesus Christ. Amen.

A Prayer of Confession for Lent or Ordinary Time (7)

Lord God, forgive us.
   Doing your will does not always flow naturally:
      Convention overshadows conviction;
      Bad habits die hard;
      Good habits form slowly.

Doing your will is not always a spontaneous choice:
Your way is sometimes unclear;
Your direction is often unpopular;
Your path is seldom profitable.
Create in us clean hearts, O God.
We pray in the name of Jesus Christ. Amen.

❧❧❧❧❧❧❧

A Prayer of Confession for Lent or Ordinary Time (8)

Lord God, forgive us:
Lost in ourselves,
we dwell endlessly
on yesterday's embarrassment, anger, and grief.
Lost in our domain,
it is hard to see
beyond yesterday's fighting, suspicion, and fear.
Lost in our fantasy,
it is tempting
to live in yesterday's illusions.
So fill us with the Spirit of Jesus Christ,
that we might be lost
in the wonder and sanity of your hope.
We pray in the name of Jesus Christ. Amen.

❧❧❧❧❧❧❧

A Prayer of Confession for Lent or Ordinary Time (9)

Lord God, forgive us:
In our words,
we are tempted to speak truth in whispered tones.
In our work,
we are tempted to serve you with halfhearted energy.
In our worship,
we are tempted to thank you with leftover gifts.

As you forgive and make us whole again,
> give us, we pray,
> > a gentle boldness,
> > a fresh chore, and
> > a new spirit within us.
We pray in the name of Jesus Christ. Amen.

ᛃᛃᛃᛃᛃᛃ

A Prayer of Confession for Lent or Ordinary Time (10)

Lord God, forgive us.
We have grown comfortable with the mundane
> and suspicious of the spectacular:
> > We work and see in it little purpose;
> > We play and see in it little pleasure;
> > We fret and see in it little point.
Startle us, we pray,
> with truth that will shake us, and
> with love that will not let us go.
We pray in the name of Jesus Christ. Amen.

ᛃᛃᛃᛃᛃᛃ

A Prayer of Confession for Lent or Ordinary Time (11)

Lord God:
> Do we leave you snickering
> > when we are smug of faith
> > and imagine we know who you are?
> Do we leave you in a huff
> > when we are careless of belief
> > and uncertain of what you wish us to do?
> Do we leave you slump-shouldered
> > when we too seldom wonder
> > who you are and what you wish?
Spirit of God:
> Come to us once more.
> We long to see again
> > the person and purpose of Christ.
> > > We pray in his name. Amen.

ᛃᛃᛃᛃᛃᛃ

A Prayer of Confession for Lent or Ordinary Time (12)

Lord God, forgive us.
Sometimes our feelings of guilt are largely pathological
    and without foundation
    save in the warps of our minds
    where truth is twisted to fit our rigid thinking.
Other times our feelings of guilt are absent
    and lost in the wrinkles of conformity
    to the way things are done
    in the places of our customary living.
Transform us, we pray,
    that by our living and moving
    we may prove
    what is the will of God
    and give evidence of your coming kingdom.
We pray in the name of Jesus Christ. Amen.

A Prayer of Confession for Lent or Ordinary Time (13)
(especially for the dog days of summer)

Come, Lord God, to make us whole
    in the slow tread of seasons
    and in the quickstep of days.
        We have let the sound of angels singing
            be muffled by engines grinding.
        We have permitted the breeze of seraphim wings
            to be stifled by pavement heat rising.
        We have allowed our vision of Christ
            to be restrained by tedious acts of living.
            Give us, Lord God, senses born of brisk belief
                that these hot days be filled
                with dancing.
            We pray in the name of Jesus Christ. Amen.

A Prayer of Confession for Lent or Ordinary Time (14)

Lord God, forgive us.
Too often we are as blind people
   following the majority:
      It is as though we see
         no ugly things
            in your beautiful world,
         no confused directions
            in your ordered creation,
         no greedy exploits
            in your loving domain.
Give us eyes to see,
   words to speak, and
   courage to see all things made new.
We pray in the name of Jesus Christ. Amen.

A Prayer of Confession for Lent or Ordinary Time (15)

Lord God, forgive our bleak imaginations
   and our dreams that refuse inspiration.
      In our hearts, our homes, and our land
         we imagine things are as they must be; so
         we dream of little more than refining what is.
Lord God, forgive our drab memories
   and our lackluster souvenirs.
      In our hearts, our homes, and our land
         we remember no help in ages past; so
         we summon no hope for years to come.
Come, Holy Spirit of God.
Lead us to your promise of the glad hour
   that shall surely come,
   glowing brightly in the shadows of the hour
   that surely now is.
We pray in the name of Jesus Christ. Amen.

A Prayer of Confession for Lent or Ordinary Time (16)

Lord God, forgive us:
    Our fear for the future
      shows neither faith nor resolve;
    Our longing for justice
      is overcome by cynicism and distrust;
    Our dread of being lonely
      is confused by self-doubt and fear of betrayal.
        Give to us a new vision, O God,
          of joining the glad company
          of the trustworthy and true
          sauntering about
          putting to shame
          the deceivers and
          the liars and
          the pretenders that all is well.
      We pray in the name of Jesus Christ. Amen.

A Prayer of Confession for Lent or Ordinary Time (17)
(especially for a Sunday near the Fourth of July)

Lord God,
    too often we find it more expedient
    to soft-shoe around and among principalities and powers
    than to trust the memory of your promises fulfilled.
      The hope of this earth is threatened by greed;
      The hope of this free people is threatened by excesses;
      The hope of each one of us is threatened by the sorrow of it all
        that accepts no comfort.
        Forgive us, O God.
        When we do not choose to remember
          your love divine all loves excelling,
          how can we be lost
          in wonder, love, and praise?
Yet, in the memory and presence of Jesus Christ,
    we pray in his name
    for your will to be done on earth
    as it is in heaven. Amen.

A Prayer of Confession for Lent or Ordinary Time (18)

Lord God, forgive our feeble efforts
   to make you over to fit our image:
      It is easier to restate your truth in easy cliches
         than it is to speak in words that change one's mind;
      It is easier to rewrite your hope in easy answers
         than it is to see through one's perplexity;
      It is easier to rethink your grace in easy pardon
         than it is to modify one's way.
By the Spirit of Jesus Christ,
   visit us with the full depth of your forgiveness
   and make us over to fit your image.
We pray in his name. Amen.

※※※※※※※

A Prayer of Confession for Lent or Ordinary Time (19)

Lord God, listen carefully to this sad confession:
   Some of us avoid all news that is bad.
   Some of us imagine there is little news that is good.
   Some days we exchange places with each other.
      Forgive our customary silence
         that says nothing and does less;
      Forgive our usual despair
         that dreams of shadows and hopes for night;
      Forgive our lingering doubt
         that wonders where you are.
         Come, Spirit of God,
            to inspire our speech,
            our vision,
            and our trust.
         We pray in the name of Jesus Christ. Amen.

※※※※※※※

A Prayer of Confession for Lent or Ordinary Time (20)

Lord God, forgive us.
   We limit our vision
      to what our eyes can see:
         A moment of joy
            or a moment of despair;

        A moment of truth
          or a moment of deception;
        A moment of harmony
          or a moment of discord.
      Do not weary of our slovenly way.
      Keep us in the promise
        of what you see:
          A new heaven
            and a new earth.
      Filled with such hope,
        give us grace for this and every moment.
      We pray in the name of Jesus Christ. Amen.

༺༺༺༺༺༺༺

A Prayer of Confession for Lent or Ordinary Time (21)
(especially for the Sunday before Labor Day)

Lord God, forgive us.
We wrap our days in a shroud of busy routine
    that protects us from the rigors of what we believe.
        Our families are left too often lonely;
        Our neighbors are left too often in need of a friend;
        Our community is left too often in need of truth; and
        Your church is left too often in need of servants.
Interrupt us with the gospel of Jesus Christ
    that our days may be filled with the work of faithfulness.
We pray in his name. Amen.

༺༺༺༺༺༺༺

A Prayer of Confession for Palm/Passion Sunday (22)

We do not fully know this Jesus
    who upsets our religious practice
    and drives from the temple of our worship
    and the temple of our hearts
    all things that profane your holy name.
We do not fully fathom this Jesus
    who does not tolerate
    our failure to do
    what we have been wondrously knit to do.

We do not fully understand this Jesus
   who teaches us in parables
   we cannot misunderstand.
      At week's beginning who will shout hosannah?
      By week's end who will shout crucify?
      Forgive our easy answers to these hard questions.
      We pray in his name. Amen.

⌇⌇⌇⌇⌇⌇⌇

A Prayer of Confession for Maundy Thursday (or Christmas Eve) (23)

Lord God,
   forgive our ignoble choices:
      Festering bitterness clouds our vision;
      Lingering fear obscures our faith;
      Nervous impatience numbs our waiting for you.
         On this night of memorial feasting,
            give us eyes to see the unfolding of your will
            and ears to hear the voices of your grace.
We pray in the name of Jesus Christ. Amen.

⌇⌇⌇⌇⌇⌇⌇

A Prayer of Confession for Maundy Thursday (24)

Lord God, forgive us.
Our innocence is lost.
We have bartered love for love
   and our world gets by, trading loyalty for loyalty.
      Sometimes we require too much
         and give too little.
      Other times we require too little
         and expect too much.
With such trading of affection and allegiance
   gospel seems complex and heavy,
      or meaningless and light.
Refresh us now
   at this banquet set
      for the memory of innocence
      and the hope of mercy.
We pray in the name of Jesus Christ. Amen.

⌇⌇⌇⌇⌇⌇⌇

A Prayer of Confession for Easter (25)

Lord God:
    We fight wars to end wars
      and war goes on;
    We pass laws to end wrong
      and wrong goes on;
    We find cures to end disease
      and disease goes on.
        Forgive us
          when we lose sight of your Easter promise.
        Forgive also
          that bitterness among us that wants no peace,
          that greed among us that wants no right, and
          that living around us that imagines no death.
        Then fill us, we pray,
          with the hope of Easter.
        We pray in the name of the living Christ. Amen.

A Prayer of Confession for Easter (26)

Forgive us, O God,
    if in the perplexity of this day
    the musing of the church should become too simple or too complex:
      Let the sound of our hymns
        echo the wonder of women who saw the empty tomb
        and remembered what they had been taught.
Forgive us, O God,
    if in the mystery of this day
    the voice of the church should be timid or frail.
      Let the sound of our proclaiming
        echo the voice of bewildered disciples
        who at last found words to speak.
Forgive us, O God,
    if after the pageantry of this day
    the memory of the church should fade or grow weary.
      Let the sound of our prayers
        echo the fearful confidence of parents and martyrs
        who worshiped in these places before us.
We pray in the name of Jesus Christ. Amen.

A Prayer of Confession for Easter or Eastertide (27)

Lord God, in the world of our living:
　　It is hard to think of any new thing
　　　　that is not a product or a service;
　　It is hard to think of any new way
　　　　that is not a reshaping or a rerouting;
　　It is hard to think of any new dimension
　　　　that is not a fantasy or a science fiction.
　　　　　　Forgive our lackluster faith
　　　　　　　　and our dull imagining.
　　　　　　Give us grace
　　　　　　　　that we might know Easter.
　　　　　　We pray in the name of Jesus Christ,
　　　　　　　　our risen Lord. Amen.

Chapter 2

Pastoral Prayers for Exiles
at Worship on the Lord's Day

A Pastoral Prayer for Advent (28)

We are a people who give names.
You made us this way, you know,
   and in this way
   you made us unique
   among all your creatures that live and breathe:
      Tree . . . elm;
      Dog . . . Labrador;
      Person . . . James William.[1]
         See what you have done?
         In naming we do our principal taming.

By what names, then, shall we name you,
   this one holy God who will not be tamed?

      Listen, we pray,
         to these names of the season
         that flow smoothly from our tongues:

            Wonderful Counselor,
            Prince of Peace.

      They are names by which we name you
         on this glad Sunday in Advent:

            Wonderful Counselor,
            Prince of Peace.

Listen to them carefully, we pray,
    but then wiggle from beneath these names,
    prop your foot on the mound of them
    and make us know you are more . . .

always more than we can imagine or name.

And yet,
  we do most humbly pray for counsel,
  counsel that is full of wonder to many in this once and
      too often proud land.
    We pray first that you give counsel
      to our president
      and all who advise and speak for him;
      and to makers and enforcers of laws
      and those who are subject to them;
      and to judges and dividers of mortal measure
      and those who make cases before them.

  Then, at last,
    when *by law* all matters are closed,
    give yet more counsel full of wonder,
    that *by grace* your light of truth
    might be seen in the dark shadows that yet circle
    all around.

That is the least of it . . .
  the penny-ante of it . . .
  the dime-a-dozen of it . . .
  the occupying-too-much-time of it.

  Come, Wonderful Counselor, Prince of peace,
    hear your people in the matters of consequence:
      The people are hungry of body and hungry of soul;
      The people are at war within and without;
      The children who have too little expect nothing;
      The children who have too much whine;
      The people who have, get;
      The people who don't have are angry;
      Too many people who know don't understand;
      Too many people who don't understand don't wish to know;
      The comfortable make us uncomfortable;
      The uncomfortable make us uneasy;

The diseases are complicated;
We always hurt the ones we love; and
The church gets lost in the bickering of its councils.

These are the matters that matter,
Wonderful Counselor, Prince of peace.
Come with your wonderful counsel
and bring us your princely peace.

These are our Advent prayers.
Thank you for listening.
As we wait for your coming,
surprise us with good answers to our deep prayers
and bring quickly the full, unadorned, extravagant hope of Christmas.
We pray in the name of Jesus Christ. Amen.

❧❧❧❧❧❧❧

A Pastoral Prayer for Advent (29)

Merciful God:

By the faith given them,
Abraham expected to establish the people of promise,
Sarah expected in her old age to give birth to a child of promise,
Noah expected to receive the olive branch of promise,
Moses expected to reach the land of promise,
prophets expected the dawn of the day of promise,
Mary expected the fullness of the Christ of promise, and
apostles expected to spread the church of promise.

Now by the faith given us,
grant that we,
with eager anticipation renewed by the season,
might catch a vision of your promise for our time
so that we shall move through these days
expecting your word to be true.

Nations rage and kingdoms totter:
    Strengthen the noble;
    Protect the innocent;
    Convict the evil in their way.
    Give the church words of truth
      and deeds of kindness.
        Come, Lord Jesus.
        Fill the church with the promise of peace on earth.[2]

The hurricanes blow, floods descend and buildings are damaged:[3]
    Console the grieving;
    Uphold the neighbors;
    Restore the victims;
    Give to the church
      words of truth and deeds of kindness.
        Come, Lord Jesus.
        Fill the church with the promise of still and calm.

Disease comes and breathing stops:
    Receive the faithful;
    Comfort the grieving;
    Bolster the caregivers;
    Give to the church
      words of truth and deeds of kindness.
        Come, Lord Jesus.
        Fill the church with the promise of no more crying.

Governments loudly groan and boldly grovel:
    Encourage the brave;
    Silence the greedy;
    Champion the good;
    Give to the church
      words of truth and deeds of kindness.
        Come, Lord Jesus.
        Fill the church with the promise of verity.

The hungry are gaunt and the homeless are cold:
    Sustain the generous;
    Heal the deranged;
    Shield the children;

Give to the church
    words of truth and deeds of kindness.
        Come, Lord Jesus.
        Fill the church with the promise of a banquet
            and many dwellings.

The holiday comes and excitement surrounds us:
    Soften the cynical;
    Surprise the hopeless;
    Seal on earth the laughter of children;
    Give to the church
        words of truth and deeds of kindness.
            Come, Lord Jesus.
            Fill the church with the promise of your kingdom
                come on earth as it is in heaven.

Not for the world and the church alone do we pray.
Without shame, we pray for ourselves.
In anticipation of the holiday, merciful God,
    we bow in longing of a new break in the old cycles.
        Give us a fresh vision of hope's advent.
        Give us memory that goes beyond war's alarm
            to see Bethlehem's stall and
            to hear angels singing
            that in this day
            we might eagerly anticipate
                the day of complete kindness,
                the day of uncompromised justice,
                the day of absolute truth,
                the day of full health,
                the day when grief shall end,
                the day when joy shall abound;

            and, until that day,
            give us grace to live kindly,
            give us grace to live justly,
            give us grace to live truth,
            give us grace to live in health of body and health of mind,
            and when health fails,
            give us grace to serve each other,
            give us grace to live in love,
            and when death comes,
            give us grace to comfort each other in the promise of life

and give us grace to know an interval of laughter
in all of our waiting.

We make these and all of our prayers
in the name of Jesus Christ. Amen.

✥✥✥✥✥✥✥

A Pastoral Prayer for Lent or Ordinary Time (30)

Merciful and steady God,
you speak and the days begin their cycle;
you breathe and our lives quicken in the days;
you arrive and our time is filled with hope.
Give us such faith, we pray,
that we may have life abundantly
and dream good dreams of what we cannot see.
In our life and in our dreams,
we have many prayers.

We pray for those, O God,
for whom the world is filled with fear:
For the children and those who nurture them;
For teens and those who guide them;
For the youthful and those who mentor them;
For the mature and those who befriend them;
For the seniors and those who listen to them.

Hide none of us, we pray,
from the reality of that which causes us to be afraid;
but allow nothing to defeat us
save the kind and steady truth you send in Jesus Christ
and in his ever present Spirit.

Lord God,
there is movement in our land and in our world:
Bitterness is speaking;
The tide of change is flowing; and
The poor are losing ground.

Give voice to those of noble vision.
Silence those of greedy spirit.
Give courage to those who speak truth.
Bring change that is right and fair.

Merciful God,
  your church feels alone and afraid
  and is here praying for itself:
    Give depth of grace to the shallow and noisy among us;
    Give humility to the spiritual proud;
    Give courage to the faithful;
    Make of us a meek and noble body of Christ.

As ever, O God,
  we pray:
    For those whose lives and homes are torn asunder;
    For those whose bodies are racked with pain;
    For those whose spirits are low slung;
    For those whose losses are hard to bear;
    For those whose loneliness is real;
    For those whose work is exhausting.
      Come, Spirit of God.
      Bring healing.

And, O God, lest we forget,
  we pray also:
    For those whose lives and homes are secure and safe;
    For those whose bodies are strong and healthy;
    For those whose joys cannot be contained;
    For those whose spirits soar with the eagles;
    For those whose relationships are healthy and pure;
    For those whose work is rewarding.
      Come, Spirit of God.
      Bring rejoicing.

Now, O God, bring peace in our time:
  peace in our church,
  peace in our homes,
  peace in our neighborhoods,
  peace in our city,
  peace in our nation, and
  peace in our world.
In the name of the Prince of peace. Amen.

A Pastoral Prayer for Lent or Ordinary Time (31)

Lord God,
    you are a troublesome mystery we can scarcely imagine
    and nowhere near fathom.
      We have no brash boldness
        that would tempt us
        to reach out and touch your raw holiness;
        and yet . . .
        and yet . . .
        Lord God:
          You are light to every dark shadow
            that closes around us;
          You are comfort to every fearsome grief
            that cripples us; and
          You are challenge to every truthful thought
            that makes us who we are.
            In Jesus the Christ,
              you touched us once,
              and in his Spirit you touch us still.
            We cannot understand the secrets of your being,
              yet you allow us to know you intimately.
            Hear our songs of praise
              and our prayers of surprise.

On this day of change in our land[4]
    we are aware of change and turmoil in many lands, O God.
      We pray for leaders in the kingdoms of the world
        and especially the kingdoms of the third world:
          Give them clear thoughts
            and pure motives;
          Give them the will to listen
            and the wisdom to select truthful advisers;
          Give them a passion to know your will
            and the courage to act on such fearful knowing.

On this day also, O God,
    we pray for enemies,
    in any corner of this beautiful and broken world.
      Some beliefs that govern
        we do not understand.
      Other such human thoughts
        we understand all too well.

Breathe upon enemies,
   theirs and ours,
   whoever they and we might be,
   a peaceful breeze
   that will soothe our burning and theirs
   whoever we and they may be.

And we pray for the church today . . .
   especially this day we pray for the church:
     Nourish within each of us the truth you have planted here.
     Pour out the Spirit of Jesus Christ on us over and over and over again.
     Make us the faithful people of God
       joined together with you
       and with our sisters and brothers
       in this congregation,
       in this community,
       and around the world.
     Give us eyes to see Christ in each other
       and in the faces of those who need us,
       that when we have served the least of these
       we will know we have served Christ.

Often in the last week or so . . .
   too often to our sure thinking and longing,
   we have gathered in this place
   and at the side of open graves
   to claim as boldly as we know how
   the promise of resurrection for those whom we have deeply loved
   and whose memory we shall long cherish.
     While we are grateful more than we know how to say
       for the promises fulfilled,
       our people,
       too many of them
       are left low-pitched with broken hearts.
         Deal gently with them, Lord God.
         Deal gently but with strength and healing.
         Fill them with the twin gifts of memory and hope.

And, now, O God,
   bless and heal those who are ill
   and those who tend them:
     [names of the ill and their caregivers to be entered here]

In this place and with these people,
>   we make all our prayers in the name of Jesus Christ. Amen.

༄༄༄༄༄༄

A Pastoral Prayer for Lent or Ordinary Time (32)

God of forever,
>   O God of eternity,
>   you have blessed us with time:
>>   A time in which to worship;
>>   A time in which to pray;
>>   A time in which to live in faith
>>>   and in faithfulness.

By your Son and by his Spirit,
>   you visit us
>   in the seasons of our lives.

Before us
>   have gone generations of your servants
>   who have tasted your love,
>   who have touched your mercy,
>   who have accepted your forgiveness, and
>   who have ventured into your purpose—
>>   Patriarch, matriarch;
>>   Leaders, judges;
>>   Servants, Savior;
>>   Apostles, martyrs, and reformers—
>>>   whose stories are preserved for us as Holy Scripture
>>>   and as history remembered.

Give us grace just now, we pray,
>   that we might be learning from those who have gone before us and
>   that we might be faithful in this and every day of our lives.

God of forever,
>   we wish to know you in a particular way in this season:
>>   The days of childhood seem long in their passing,
>>>   like Christmas too slow in its coming.
>>>>   Yet now, O God, for some and soon for all,
>>>>>   the days of childhood are but as yesterday.
>>   The days of youth
>>>   were filled with dreams and ideals

when both body and spirit seemed invincible.
　Yet now, O God, for some and soon for everyone,
　　invincibility fades and we grow weary.
The days of adulthood
　move at breakneck speed
　as we move headlong into fragile.
　　Yet it is now, O God,
　　　in this glad day,
　　　when we have come to pray
　　　for the sweet gift
　　　of those things which remain:
　　　　We pray for faith.
　　　　We pray for hope.
　　　　We pray for love,
　　　　　and the greatest of these
　　　　　really is love.
And we pray for the church
　in which we live out these things that remain.
And we pray for the world
　out of which you have called us to be the church.
Help us, we pray,
　to be faithful in the church,
　that the wounds of our spirits might be bound
　and the wounds of the world might be healed.

In this time that passes so quickly, we pray
　that wars shall soon end,
　that fear shall soon be calmed,
　that broken hearts shall soon be mended,
　that diseases shall soon be healed,
　that the hungry shall soon be fed,
　that the homeless shall soon find a place,
　that the restless shall soon find peace,
　that the addicted shall soon find freedom,
　that grief shall soon pass away, and
　that joy and laughter shall have their day.

By your Holy Spirit, O God,
　make us willing answers to the prayers we make.
All of our prayers are in the name of Jesus Christ our Lord. Amen.

A Pastoral Prayer for Lent or Ordinary Time (33)

God of mercy and of grace
   you have spoken in voices loud and voices small.
      Listen now,
         not to the deserving of our voices,
         but to the yearning of our hearts.
God of truth and of grace,
   by the strength of your voice the earth gives life.
      Listen now,
         not to the strength of our demands,
         but to the passion of our longings.
God of wisdom and of grace,
   by the Spirit of Christ your Word echoes in this people.
      Listen now,
         not to the logic of our cases argued
         but to the hope of our belief that you hear us.

We pray for the church, O God:

In our prayers for the church
   we long sometimes for simpler days gone now
   when church seemed more an accepted part of daily life and routine.
      Give us grace to reclaim the good in that memory
         and wisdom to meet the challenges of this day.
         The world is more complex now, as is living in these days.
         As a congregation of your people, keep us dreaming.
         We want to be
            a voice for truth,
            a place of justice,
            a balm of healing,
            a sanctuary of mercy,
            a people of nurture
               where children are seen as signs of your kingdom,
               where noble ideals are fostered in the days of youth,
               where faithfulness is encouraged among adults, and
               where the wisdom of long years is cherished.
         Come, Holy Spirit of Christ,
            move among us,
             that in these days
            when it is so easy not to be the church
            we might be your brave and faithful people.

Not for the church alone, O God,
   but for the world we also pray:

      We are grateful for leaders
         who long in their deliberation
         to do your will.
            Fill them with grace and strength in their conviction.
            In matters that divide persons of goodwill,
               give patience and understanding
               and direction.

      We find on all sides of the streets we drive
         people who are afraid,
         people who are angry, and
         people who are afraid and angry;
         but also
         we see signs of goodwill and hope.
            Restore this community
               to a place of security and fair play.

      We recognize around the world in the pictures we see
         people whose lives are shattered by war and famine,
         and people whose lives are racked with pain and disease;
         but also
         we see signs of peace and plenty and healing.
            Restore this good earth
               to a place of peace and goodwill among all people.

Hear now our prayers
   for those who grieve,
   for those who are anxious,
   for those who are lonely,
   for those who are tired,
   for those who are confused,
   for those who are addicted,
   for those who are guilty.
      Give us grace
         to be answers to the prayers we make.
      We pray in the name of Jesus Christ. Amen.

A Pastoral Prayer for Lent or Ordinary Time (34)

Merciful God:
   With our eyes,
      when we look reverently,
      we see the splendor and finest features
      of your creation.
   With our ears,
      when we listen with intensity,
      we hear the symphony and still voice
      of your passing by.
   With our hearts,
      when we believe with the dreamers,
      we feel the warmth and strength
      of your love.
   With our minds,
      when we think beyond our knowing
      to the thoughts of your spirit,
      we know you are God.

     Come, then, Holy Spirit of Christ,
        attend our praying,
        not because we presume to speak to the Holy One,
        but because you, holy and gracious God,
        have promised to listen.
           We claim now that promise.

The stormy chaos of our lives billows.
Come to us, Spirit of Christ.
We're praying for hope in our time.

   Come to us, Lord Jesus.
   Over the fray of lust for political power,
      cast the calm of noble conviction.

   Come to us, Lord Jesus.
   Over the strife between races and clans,
      cast the tranquillity of understanding.

   Hold out your hand to us, Lord Jesus.
   Over hate born of desperation,
      cast the composure of plenty.

Over fear born of living in the presence of indifference,
    cast the healing balm of love.

Over worry born of greed,
    cast the poise of generosity.

Come to us, Lord Jesus.
Over the dismay of growing old,
    cast the satisfaction of wisdom from above

Hold out your hand to us, Lord Jesus.
Over the anxiety of grown-up responsibility,
    cast the assurance of your strength.

Over the impatience of youth,
    cast the hope of making things better.

There is more, Lord Jesus.
Over the terror of being known as we are,
    cast the mantle of your gentle acceptance.

Over tensions among people who love each other,
    cast the relief of dependable forgiveness.

Over the reality of disease,
    cast the touch of your steady healing.

Over the dread of dying,
    cast always the hope of living.

We make all of our prayers
    in the name of Jesus Christ. Amen.

ᏩᏩᏩᏩᏩᏩ

A Pastoral Prayer for Easter (35)

Lord God,
    for whom time and eternity are woven like a mantle
    and for whom space and infinity are knit like a shawl,
    to our way of thinking, you know more than everything:
    more even than *everything*.

In honesty,
  sometimes we wish you knew considerably less than that;
  but you make us this way, you know:

  Prone to dark vain ventures at being like God.

Still and yet,
  in this moment of worship,
  in this moment of reverence of a particular sort,
  in this moment when we are together before you
  singing hymns and anthems old and new,
  reading and hearing ancient texts,
  proclaiming and hearing fresh truth,
  and praying honest and hopeful Easter prayers:

in this moment of worship,
we are glad you know all that you know.
  You know the world in all its minute and vast wonder,
    scarred and broken here and there.[5]
  You know the heart of each one and of the masses,
    scarred and broken here and there.
  You know the good that mortals have done and shall yet do,
    scarred and broken here and there.
  You know the truth that is known and shall yet come to light,
    scarred and broken here and there.
  You know the passions within many for just and right causes,
    scarred and broken here and there.
  You know the memory of hope and the hope of memory,
    scarred and broken here and there.
  You know the faith of the ages in things not seen,
    scarred and broken here and there.
  You know the loves we have each known,
    scarred and broken here and there.
  You know the love of Christ Jesus,
    scarred and broken and redeemed on Calvary
    and again and again and again here and there
    and at last everywhere.

    These are the things that come to mind just now
      that we are glad you know:
      these and more that we do not just now imagine
      and more still that are beyond our imagining.

We pray with the passion of the starving
    that you give us joy in the great good of it all,
    that you cover quickly the scarring left in it all, and
    that you mend in time the yet broken of it all.

We are glad for these moments of grand Easter prayers.
Since, however,
    you listen each time we pray,
    you know full well most of our praying,
    Easter or no,
    is far less lofty.

    Bless each one who,
        no matter where else he or she may live,
        lives also in the heart of someone in this worship.
    Bless the work and the play and the rest
        of each one in this worship.
    Bless the health or the longing for health
        of each one in this worship.
    Bless the love that is felt
        by each one in this worship.
    Bless the church in its coming together,
        each one with all in the joy of this worship,
        and keep us bound to the Spirit of the risen Christ
        to those gathered now to him,
        to each other, and
        to the faithful of every land and generation.

        Bring healing to those who are ill,
            to those who are hungry,
            to those who are homeless, and
            to those who grieve.

        Bring joy to those who are just now knowing love,
            to those who have loved for many glad seasons,
            and to those who cherish the strong memory of love.

All of this we pray in the name of Jesus Christ,
    who lives and reigns with you and the Holy Spirit. Amen.

A Pastoral Prayer for the Sunday
before the Martin Luther King Jr. Holiday (36)

God whose name is I AM,
    whose will is the right wrapped in a mantle of mercy,
    whose resolve is the good infused with grace, and
    whose being is love made flesh for a season,
    your love lives still in the church
    in measures that vary by case,
    and the church comes now to pray.
        Our prayers are limited by the expanse of words.
        At a level our words are no more than
            images rising in random order from the mind,
            thoughts warmed or cooled in the heart,
            sounds rolling from the twists of tongue,
            shapes formed of lines on the page.
        At another level our words declare
            who you made us to be,
            what you give us to believe, and
            that which we dare to hope.
            Come, then, Word of God,
                listen to these words,
                and by your Spirit
                form of them a prayer.

This day,
    this very day,
    we make this place of worship
    a place of particular welcome.[6]
        Fill us with grace and energy.
        Open our hearts as we open our doors.
        The bridges have been built in our town.
        Use this occasion for the crossing of those bridges.
        Hear our prayers of thanksgiving for the gospel of truth
            that binds people of faith
            in love that transcends boundaries.
        Bless this strong messenger
            and the faithful congregation he serves.

This day,
    this very day,
    peace on many fronts seems near and possible
    and yet far, far away.

Be with those who talk for reconciliation
 that they may speak truth in mercy.
Give them the will to listen
 that they may hear the depth of bitterness born of pain.
Be with those whose lives are snuffed or left in shambles
 as talking grinds on and on and on and on.

This day,
 this very day,
 people the whole world over
 are fearful of meals that will not be
 for children who do not know why.
  Be with those
   by whose slip of the tongue markets rise and fall
   or by whose indiscretions jobs are lost
   and by whose hard hearts bounty goes unshared.
  Tame all such fearsome power
   and make it clean . . . very, very clean,
   as with a refiner's white-hot fire.

This day,
 this very day,
 the news of disease is fearful and cruel.
  Make strong and real all threads of hope.
  Give new insights to those who bear the gift of healing.
  Give courage and strength to those who are ill
   and to those who care for them.

This day,
 this very day,
 grief is fresh and grief is heavy.
  Heal these wounds.
  Give visions of place beyond place and time beyond time
   even as you fill this time and this place
   with purpose and hope.

This day,
 this very day,
 by the millions of millions,
 those who will
 shall taste, and smell, and see, and hear, and touch
 the mystery of loving and of being loved.

How wondrous are your ways, O God.
In the wonder of your way,
    make of us the answer to our prayers.
Our prayers,
    every one of them,
    are made in the name of Jesus Christ.
Amen.

꙰꙰꙰꙰꙰꙰

A Pastoral Prayer for a Sunday in Early Spring (37)

God of life and of beauty,
    with the breath of our days
    drawn from your considerable majesty
    we come to speak prayers of deep praise and vigorous beseeching.
        Blend, then, the throbbing sounds of all our hearts
            with the raucous silence of all our thinking
            that the voice of this one
            might be both bold and humble
            in speaking the prayer of these many.
        More than that, O God of each one of us,
            grant that the unspoken prayers,
            tucked in some secret fold of human spirit
            and brought from the clamor and quiet of many places,
            might, in your imposing Spirit, be heard
            as the prayer of us all.

In the order of life, death, and new life,
    we are surrounded just now
    with delicate splendor.
        The earth is just beginning to bring forth vegetation
            poised on the verge of bursting
            to declare your glory.
        The creatures great and small
            are just beginning to return with ardor
            like our own
            to sing your praise.
                Hear our thanks, O God of all creation,
                    and feel our gratitude
                    for the gift of life
                    that is just on the edge of new
                    even in the most seasoned among us.

You have blessed this glad assembly
> with much hope borne on the wings of the very young
> and lived in brave and playful innocence.
>   Bless the children, we pray,
>   and give us grace to be with them the church.

You have blessed us also
> with persons of wisdom borne on the wings of years
> and lived in faithful devotion and service.
>   Bless them all, we pray,
>   and give the church grace to listen.

Yet, O most merciful God,
>   even as we applaud with energy
>   the twin gifts of new life and wisdom,
>   we know there are many among us
>   who look closely just now
>   into Death's cold and craggy eye
>   as Death backs out the door clutching our own
>   or lurking nearby.
>   Fill us all with hope
>   beyond what we can see
>   through this clouded glass.
>   Fill us also with strong and tender grace
>   that we might bring healing
>   to those who keep vigil
>   and to those whose grief is fresh and deep.

Our news is filled just now
>   with stories of horror that sound too familiar.[7]
>   Be near those who grieve
>   the senseless death of children.
>   Be near those whose violent acts
>   are borne of something ugly which we do not understand.
>   Be near the ones who must try to make sense
>   of that which is so utterly senseless.
>   Be near us all, O God of all knowing,
>   lest we become so accustomed to such news
>   that it should begin to make sense
>   in its very commonplace.

In our prayers for the church, O God,
>   our emotions turn quickly from dark dread

to a strange and sure hope
drawn carefully from your promises,
which we are wont to trust.
   It is true, of course,
      in many bright places and dark, dark crannies
      the church groans through its days
      in half-blind searching for direction
      through a maze of indelicate issues.
   Still,
      truth is being preached in the name of Jesus,
      wounds are being healed in the name of Jesus,
      despair is being challenged in the name of Jesus,
      greed is being shamed in the name of Jesus,
      tyrants are being faced down in the name of Jesus,
      people are laughing and praying and singing in the name of Jesus.
        In these and more
           we dare to breathe deep sighs of relief.
   As you have guided the church
      through days of fullness in purpose
      and days of perplexity,
      so guide the church again and again and again
      and yet again
      until the whole church is faithful to your call.

As ever, O God,
   we pray for peace
      and for those who work for it;
   we pray for the ill
      and for those who tend them;
   we pray for the lonely
      and for those who befriend them;
   we pray for the anxious
      and for those who assure them;
   we pray for the frightened
      and for those who encourage them;
   we pray for the glad of heart
      and for those who laugh with them.
      Give grace to us all, O God.
      We pray in the name of Jesus Christ. Amen.

A Pastoral Prayer for the Sunday before Memorial Day (38)

Lord God,
    for what on this day do we pray?
        You know us better than we know ourselves.
        You know the secret longings of our hearts.
        You know our thoughts before we think them.
        You know our prayers in their unspoken honesty, and
            you know them in their stated ritual.
                Hear us, then,
                    and, by your Holy Spirit,
                    help us give honorable form
                    to all our prayers:
                    those spoken and
                    those known only to you.

On this the eve of the day set aside for a memorial,
    as a people,
  we have set the flags flying.
      We do remember.
      For some the memory is fresh and gaping.
      For some the memory is distant but vivid.
      For some the memory is lived as in a history text.
      For all of us,
          when we think of it,
          we remember and we are grateful:

          grateful . . . deeply, deeply grateful
          for the dedication of those brave men and women
          whose sacrifice to just cause
          is immeasurable . . .
          quite immeasurable.

You have chosen the church,
      as people of God,
      to keep the memory in a particular way
      until that glad day
      for which we hold the certain hope
      when all wars shall end
      and there shall be no more pain or sorrow
      and tears shall be no more.

Because that is so,
in these hard years that intervene,
we pray for ourselves.
Temptations range
from the lure of shady dealing
to the urge to deep despair.
You have chosen us to know the Spirit of Jesus Christ
to cleanse and sustain.
We live in a world that ranges
from the unimaginably beautiful
to the unthinkably brutal.
You have chosen us to teach the truth of Jesus Christ
to support and heal.
We live among people who range
from the extraordinarily kind
to the curiously evil.
You have chosen to give us the grace of Jesus Christ,
that our lot and influence be cast with the kind.

From the memory of Christ
and in the presence of Christ's Holy Spirit,
fill us with the hope of this and every day
to the end, O God,
that soon, very, very soon,
there will be no further need
for human sacrifice
in the cause of freedom and justice for all
and the sacrifices of those whose memory
we honor tomorrow
will not have been in vain.

We're bold to pray for more.
We pray for the world.
The pictures that flood our family rooms every evening
and those tossed on our doorsteps each morning
leave us to wring our hands.
We surely do not understand all the issues,
but we are sure there is some dark prejudice
or some blind insanity
or some lurking evil
that breeds inhumanity.

We do not know what to do,
   and so we pray:
   with all our hearts we pray.
     First we pray
       you will cast your light of truth
       on any vestige of a shadow of dark prejudice
       lurking yet in the cobwebs of our souls.
     Then we pray for those
       with power and influence to correct evil
       and power to set people free.

And we pray for the church, O God.
Make us strong,
   not that we may boast
   but that we might serve the more.
Make us open to your Spirit
   working in each one of us and
   working among all of us
   that we might be,
   for many and for each other,
   the body of Jesus Christ here in this place
   and in the places we live and work and play.
Bind us together
   with the church
   as it exists in places where it is not easy to be the church:
   where truth cannot be freely spoken
   and kindness cannot be simply expressed.
     Give to our sisters and brothers
       the strength and courage of their faith.

And now, O God, we pray
   that you will heal those who are ill,
   that you will comfort those who grieve,
   that you will befriend those who are lonely,
   that you will calm those who are troubled,
   that you will mend the hearts that are broken, and
   that you will make us answers
     to the prayers we make this and every day.
       We pray in the name of Jesus Christ. Amen.

A Pastoral Prayer for the Meeting of the General Assembly (39)

O God whose power is love
   and whose love is power,
   whose name is I AM
   and whose being is Word made flesh,
   listen carefully now,
   listen ever so carefully
   to the firm words with which we form
   our considerable prayers . . .
   our prayers of the heart and
   our prayers of the mind.
     We are together at worship.
     Sometimes we worship alone in the quiet of home
        with no more sound than the refrigerator whirring in the kitchen
        or the sprinkler swishing in the yard.
     Sometimes we worship alone in the din of the crowd
        to the tune of horns blaring
        or to the litany of daily dealing;

     but today . . .
     today we are together . . .
     together in this secure and dangerous place
     of our habitual worship.
Today we join our voices to the glad and pleading chorus
     of the many who here have prayed before us.
Like them,
     we pray with all the bold humility we know how to muster.
Just so,
     just so, God of love and power,
     we do not pray that you deliver us from danger,
     we pray you deliver us from evil.

     The hosts surround us, O God:
        Too much good from science
           has gone mad;
        Too much nobility from government of the people
           has gone shallow;
        Too much the tried and true
           has given over to change;
        Too much the old and worn
           has refused to change;

> Too much the neighbors
> have gone to war;
> Too much entertainment
> has gone greedy;
> Too much the church
> seeks thin answers to wrong questions.

> Do not deliver us, we pray once more,
> from the press of these very present dangers.
> Deliver us, rather, from faithlessness
> in the presence of such pressing dangers.

Lord God of the church,
the General Assembly of our denomination
is meeting this week.
> Inspire the commissioners and observers
> not so much with the grandness of it all
> as with Spirit that inspires such grand ceremony.
> Deliver the commissioners and observers
> not so much from controversy
> as from the narrow vision that sees no faithfulness
> in those of differing opinion.
> Fill the commissioners and observers
> not so much with jealousy of opinion
> as with the burning desire to do your will
> in matters large and small.

> Above all, O God,
> deliver the church from further division.

Merciful God,
> bring healing to the sick,
> bring comfort to the grieving,
> bring friends to the lonely,
> bring rest to the weary,
> bring calm to the anxious,
> bring food to the hungry,
> bring place to the homeless,
> bring forgiving to the estranged,
> bring peace to the conflicted,
> bring joy to the young,
> bring satisfaction to the old, and
> bring thankfulness to us all.

The gift of thankfulness rests strangely,
 as in a nest,
 near the cockles and strings of our hearts.
  We pray in the name of Jesus Christ. Amen.

☙☙☙☙☙☙☙

A Pastoral Prayer for Promotion Day (40)

God of the sea
 and of all that swim;
God of the sky
 and of all that soar;
God of the earth
 and of all who run,
 and dance,
 and strut,
 and saunter,
 and limp,
 and wheel,
 and jive,

 This is your people speaking,
  gathered here in this old sanctuary
  where so many before us have gathered to pray.
 Do not weary of listening,
  because there is quite a lot more we wish to say.

Thank you.
We begin with thank you.
 Thank you on this glad promotion day
  for the youngest among us,
  who learn by the soft feel and rhythms
  of your old, old story,
  given to us for a season.
 Thank you
  for the yard children,
  who learn by brave play and noisy listening
  to your old, old story,
  given to us to join for all time.
 Thank you for those rushing headlong to the edge of adulthood,
  who learn by straining at and against
  your old, old story,
  given to us to question and push.

Thank you, O thank you,
   for those hardworking adults,
   who learn by testing in market and home
   the truth of your old, old story,
   given to us to test.
Thank you, a hundred times over, thank you
   for those whose minds and memories now crowded with years
   yet hunger to know more
   of your old, old story,
   given to us for rest.

   More than all else, on this day,
      we thank you for those who teach in the school of the church
      and those who lead those who teach in the school of the church.

Having thanked you sincerely,
   there are now some blessings
   for which we strongly
   and reverently
   and hopefully pray:

   Bless those for whom grief is fresh
      and those for whom sorrow lingers long.
   Bless those annoyed with pesky illness
      and those who do daily battle with grave disease.
   Bless those who relish the joy of friendship
      and those who long to mend broken trusts.
   Bless those who live in homes filled mostly with warm laughter
      and those who live mostly in cold tension.
   Bless those whose homes are destroyed by war
      and those working night and day to end war's alarm.
   Bless those who are hungry
      and those who feed them.
   Bless those who are homeless
      and those who shelter them.
   Bless those in high office
      and those who honor or shame them as need may arise.

   We pray in the name of Jesus Christ. Amen.

A Pastoral Prayer for Peacemaking Sunday (41)

Lord God,
    to your way of being,
    a thousand years are but as yesterday
    when it is passed,
    or so the psalmist said
    and we surely believe.
        Our slow-tread days
            are numbered mostly in tens and ones
            and pass at breakneck speed.

And yet,
    and yet,
    on this short day,
    set aside for the purpose,
    we pray.
With all the bold humility we can muster,
    we pray for peace
    where deep conflict has raged for four thousand years
    in the land we call holy
    and for what seems nearly that long
    among those in other lands
    who bear your name under different banners.
In your way of being,
    it has, in the long instance,
    lasted but four short days
    and, in the others,
    less than a day;
    but to our way of being,
    we are weary of it all.

      Show us the end.
      Show us the peaceful end.
      Show us your kingdom on earth
        as it is in heaven.[8]

Lord God,
    with your strong eyes
    you see beyond time and place,
    and yet,
    and yet,
    no falling sparrow escapes your care.

We the people are a people of every stripe and color,
    gathered in,
    from the low roads mostly
    of the far corners of the earth,
    to form what we call the "melting pot."
The brew is curdling
    with new separation
    born largely of fear and suspicion
    turned too quickly to anger.
Stir us again, we pray, as a people,
    not to make us alike
    but to make us trusting
    and each one . . .
    each one of us
    worthy of trust.

> *Show us the end.*
> *Show us the peaceful end.*
> *Show us your kingdom on earth*
>   *as it is in heaven.*

Lord God,
    for longer than we can imagine,
    you have been forming and reforming
    your people of faith.

    From the call of Abraham and Sarah,
        to the freedom march of Moses and Miriam,
        to the house of David and Bathsheba,
        to the call of Mary, Joseph, shepherds, and wise men,
        to the call of Lydia and Paul,
        you have called the likes of us to be yours.

    And yet,
        and yet,
        in this fearful day,
        many people in the church are sharply divided,
        with factions at the edges and very near the center
        passionately sure they know your will
        as they discern your will in Holy Scripture
        too often turned to unholy purpose.

Show us the end.
Show us the peaceful end.
Show us your kingdom on earth
as it is in heaven.

Lord God,
    when you wondrously made us in your image,
    you made us to live with each other
    as we live our covenant with you.
        We are sisters and brothers or
            we are husbands and wives or
            we are parents and children or
            we are friends and neighbors or
            we are some combination of these.

    And yet,
        and yet,
        we betray and are betrayed
        by the ones we love.

Show us the end.
Show us the peaceful end.
Show us your kingdom on earth
as it is in heaven.

Now we pray as we always pray:
    make well the ill,
    make calm the anxious,
    make still the grieving,
    make rested the tired.
        We pray in the name of Jesus Christ. Amen.

☙☙☙☙☙☙☙

A Pastoral Prayer for Peacemaking Sunday (42)
(following a natural disaster)

O Lord our God,
    the winds have blown from every known direction,
    floods have risen to unknown heights,
    the earth has shaken from beneath its shallow crust,[9]
    community has united in the Spirit of Christ,
    and we have seen, heard, felt, tasted, and smelled
    your dreadful and comforting presence.

Neighbors a short distance on all sides
　　and neighbors far, far away
　　labor beneath unimagined loads of rebuilding,
　　and we have come together in caring and in praying,
　　in giving and in sharing the load.
We are here because there is no place else we dare to be;
　　and we are here because there is no place else we wish to be.
As we heard you speak in the storm's dark night,
　　give us ears to hear you speak
　　in a still, small voice,
　　that our will and our strength
　　be given in your service,
　　that in the end they will say,
　　God was in this place,
　　God was in this people,
　　by this people God has brought healing.
O Lord God,
　　though the storm has struck here
　　and the earthquake there,
　　the world groans on
　　and, on this day set aside for the purpose,
　　we pray your blessing on the peacemakers:
　　Where there is illness,
　　　　give kindness to those who bring healing.[10]
　　Where there is anguish of soul,
　　　　give tender strength to those who console.
　　Where grief is fresh,
　　　　give strength to those who comfort.
　　Where there is stress in our homes,
　　　　give confidence to those who bridge differences.
　　Where there is tension in our town,
　　　　give voice to those of fair intention.
　　Where there is division in our state,
　　　　give words to those who see a greater vision.
　　Where there is bickering in our nation's capital,
　　　　give courage to those of character.
　　Where there is prejudice among the races,
　　　　give endurance to those who see beauty in color.
　　Where civil wars fester and rage,
　　　　give tenacity to those who value another's clan.
　　Where tyrants reign,
　　　　give conviction to those who speak truth.

Where there is conflict among the nations,
give discernment to those who seek accord.
Where life and home are shattered by flood and earthquake,
give stamina to those who bring relief.
And, O Lord our God,
where your church struggles to find itself,
give us a vision of the Prince of Peace
that we might aid in the answer
to all the prayers we dare to make.
We pray in the name of Jesus Christ. Amen.

༺ⱭⱭⱭⱭⱭⱭⱭ༻

A Pastoral Prayer for the Sunday before Thanksgiving (43)

Lord God,
so full of wonder,
so full of grace,
so full of mercy,
Lord God of power and of kindness,
Lord God of justice and of forgiveness,
Lord God of the order in your speaking,
present in the chaos of our making,
listen carefully to the case we build in our praying.

We the people creep forward
toward a day set by decree
as a national day of thanksgiving.
We the people also slow-tread our way as never before
to name the one
who, for a season,
will be the most powerful mortal
on the face of the earth.[11]
As a matter of national first thanks, then,
we are grateful
there are no tanks in the streets of Florida,
there is no threat of tanks in the streets of Florida, and
there appears no need for tanks in the streets of Florida.
We are, then, thankful
for those who went before
to form this government of the people
and for those who today govern with
some necessary pretension of civility.

With heads bowed just now in portentous prayer,
    we who are of the church,
    who are also of we the people,
    come to make a case before you.
Great God of truth,
  we pray you will move in these days
  amid the decision makers.
    Use the very existence of all their confused indecision
      to inspire such nobile humility
      in both of the frail contenders for the office of president
      that we the people shall soon be able
      to support the one who is winner
      or, if necessary,
      how, in your strong name,
      we shall call his flimsy hand.

That is the rugged, rough-edged case we put before you.
It makes good sense to us, but,
  as in all matters large and small,
  we bow to your ordered wisdom.

As persons of faith, however,
  the matter of thanksgiving is never first or last
  or at all mostly
  an imperial concern:
    Mostly we are thankful that before you all human power pales.
    Mostly we are thankful that you have not hidden yourself from us.
    Mostly we are thankful that you call us by name.
    Mostly we are thankful that you visit us in the Spirit of Christ.
    Mostly we are thankful that you call us out and call us the church.
    Mostly we are thankful that you set before us a banquet day by day.
    Mostly we are thankful that you show us the face of Jesus
      in the least among us.
    Mostly we are thankful that you invite us to join in your mission
      among the boisterous, frail Caesars of our season.
        In light of such thankfulness,
          we make before you the easy case
          that you move among your thankful people in this hour
          that there will be deep commitment in our acts
          of grateful dedication.

And now:

    For some, there will be freshly empty places at this year's
        Thanksgiving table.
      Treat gently their broken hearts.[12]

    For some, illness is a nuisance or, by case, a grave threat.
      Treat tenderly their suffering.

    For some, the days are too long, or by estate, too short.
      Treat sensitively their time.

    For some, love is new each day or, by necessity, a distant
        and dear memory.
      Treat warmly their bliss.

    For some, making peace is a matter of family, or by degree,
        of tribes and nations.
      Treat sympathetically their noble efforts.

    For some, believing is a matter of ease, or by circumstance,
        great struggle.
      Treat graciously our unbelief.

      We pray in the name of Jesus Christ,
        our worthy advocate
        in whom we sincerely believe. Amen.

Chapter 3

Great Prayers of Thanksgiving for Exiles at Worship

A Great Prayer of Thanksgiving (44)

We give thanks to you, O God.
By your word spoken,
   worlds are put into their orbit.
By your voice in the garden,
   our sin is laid bare.
By the telling of sure belief,
   our forebears begin our journey.
By the call of prophets,
   our paths are set straight.
By the Word made flesh,
   our hope is made complete.
In gratitude we bring gifts of bread and wine
    with the strong prayer
    that of these gifts you will spread a feast
    at which we shall know the healing of Christ.

    We pray in his name. Amen.

༄༄༄༄༄༄༄

A Great Prayer of Thanksgiving (45)

God who made everything lovely,
God who is making things lovely again,
God who keeps us dreaming lovely visions distant and near,
    as we regard the extravagant taste of the feast set before us,
    we pray you will listen slowly
    and savor the rich taste of our thanks.

We join our prayers with the prayers of
   matriarch and patriarch long and recently gone.
We join our prayers with the prayers of
   freedom marchers long and recently resting.
We join our prayers with the prayers of
   prophets and preachers long and recently at peace.
We join our prayers with the prayers of
   disciples and martyrs long and recently laughing.

Thanks flow freely at this table, King Jesus.
Thanks flow freely because we know you are right here,
   scars showing, showing scars,
   grinning big,
   ready to touch again, and
   ready to heal again, and
   ready to comfort again, and
   ready to disturb again.
      To our sure belief and practice
         you are here not in wine made blood
         and bread made flesh
         but in truth that is final
         and in truth that is real.

Thank you, Truth of God.
O thank you.
Sit with us now at this table
   and shamelessly relish our blessing.

We're praying in your name, you know.
We do all our praying in your holy name. Amen.

⫘⫘⫘⫘⫘

A Great Prayer of Thanksgiving (46)

Great and loving God,
   there are no spirits at this table so holy as your Holy Spirit,
   but there are many other spirits here with us, you know,
   and we are grateful for the thought of each and every one:
      There is the spirit of Abraham here,
         chin set toward your promise,
         and of Sarah laughing all the way.

There is the spirit of Moses here,
    staff in one hand and tablet in the other,
    and of Rahab dressed in her bangles and beads ready to rescue.
There is the spirit of Jeremiah here
    with fire in his mouth,
    and of Gomer with the taste of being forgiven in hers.
There is the spirit of King David here
    with a sling to slay the giants,
    and of Bathsheba here to tame the king.
There is the spirit here of Simon and the others
    with their late but strong belief,
    and of Mary Magdalene who was the very first to believe.
        These are all present at the table in spirit,
            plus the spirit of apostles, martyrs, and reformers
            more than we can name or number.
        When we think of it,
            it's quite a company with whom we cavort and feast
            and laugh and pray our prayer of great thanks.
        Bless this rich and savory food
            that it will nourish us soon and again
            in the clear memory of it all,
            and join us now and again
            to the Holy Spirit of Jesus
            seated in truth just there and again
            to know we are deeply thankful.

        We do most sincerely pray in his name. Amen.

Chapter 4

Prayers for Other Times
the Exiles Are Gathered for Worship

A Pastoral Prayer for an Advent Service of Lessons and Carols (47)

Lord our God,
    once long, long ago,
    at just the right time,
    you sent your Son, King of kings,
    Lord of lords,
    Prince of peace,
    to live among us.
      The season now begun,
        though it is a season of eager anticipation,
        calls us to a flood of long memory
        that flows as freely as any known spring
        cascading through winter snow.
      The memories are of stories often told
        of angels singing
        and of shepherds and kings arriving.
      The memories are also of stories of other seasons often told
        of family and friends
        and of carol singing.
          Of the latter,
            most are warm and joyful,
            but others are of empty places at the table.

Our Advent prayer
    is that you will bring all these memories together
    to move your brave people
    to the edge of promise
    in the places of home and work and worship
    that we might wait with purpose

and find joy in the time of waiting.
We pray in his name. Amen.

* * *

An Advent Litany for a Service of Lessons and Carols (48)

Lord God of new beginnings,
in the first few steps of this new beginning,
make these stumbling words our Advent litany:
where there is unrestrained joy,
give us the hope of friends in Christ with whom to share it;[1]
where there is pressing loneliness,
give us the hope of a community of Christ's caring people;
where there is growling hunger of body,
give us the hope of a great banquet with Christ at table's head;
where there is a craving hunger of mind,
give us the hope of the truth of Christ;
where there is desperate hunger of spirit,
give us the hope of deep belief in Christ;
where there is smoldering anger,
give us the hope of Christ's kindness;
where there is hard fear,
give us the hope of safety in Christ;
where there are children of plenty and children of want,
give us the hope of coming to Christ;
where there are young of innocence and young of rage,
give us the hope of Christ's ideals;
where there are elders noble and elders vile,
give us the hope of Christ's wisdom;
where there is doubt,
give us faith to see beyond what eyes can see
to the Christ who was and is and shall surely be.
Be with us now
in our hearing and singing.
In the name of Christ. Amen.

* * *

A Pastoral Prayer for Christmas Eve (49)

For what do we pray on this holy night, O God?
Is it for some new miracle?
Is it for some new marvel?
Is it for some new blessing?
Is it for some new sensation?
We pray more, O God,
    far, far more,
    that what we remember this night
    might for us again be new.
        Bless, then, to our memory, O God,
            the picture of angels and of a manger . . .
            the picture of shepherds and wise men . . .
            the picture of Mary and Joseph and the babe . . .
                oh yes, the babe.
        Bless the memory of the story, O God,
            that again we add the saga of our days
            to its ancient promise.

For whom, now, shall we stumble about
    and pray for them
    to wonder at the blessing you hold
    on the near side of fresh giving?

    Just these, so listen carefully:

    We pray for the children, O God.
    First we pray for the children
        who wiggle and whisper
        beside and all around us
        with the glad sounds of Christmas.
            Keep them safe.
            Through their watchful anticipation
                infect us all
                deeply.

    We pray also, O God,
        for those for whom merry Christmas
        is a dim memory
        or a deep sadness.

Give to them, O God,
   the healing Spirit of Christ,
   that they may feel this night
   a warm blanket of comfort.

We pray most briefly
   and yet most deeply
   for this night's great majority
   for whom peace on earth
   and a banquet feast
   are unimaginable . . .
   quite beyond imagining.
      Give them, we pray,
         some glimmer of what we see.
      Give them a dream this night
         of a peaceable kingdom,
         and keep us slow-treading in lockstep
         toward that sure day,
         gathering the broken in our arms
         along the way.

Bless those who grieve
   and those who are ill
   and those who are lonely
   and those who are afraid
   and those who tend them through this long night.
      We pray in the name of Jesus Christ. Amen.

꘎꘎꘎꘎꘎꘎

A Pastoral Prayer for Ash Wednesday (or Lent) (50)
(based on 2 Corinthians 5:20–21)

Lord God,
   whatever does it mean
   that you have made sin
   of him who knew no sin?
We don't like
   what we think that means.
      We don't like it at all.
      At least,
         we don't like what we're almost sure it means.

We're more comfortable
   when everyone gets what they deserve:
     That is,
       everyone but us
       and the ones we love
       and even for us
       we understand things better when fair is fair
       rather than when mercy is mercy.

And yet,
   except for your mercy
   what claim have we:
     to the rising of the sun,
     to the falling of the rain,
     to the taste of good food,
     to the breath of life,
     to the tug of love,
     to the freedom of thought,

     to the comfort of faith?

How much less, then,
   except for your mercy,
   have we any claim on your forgiveness.
     But that you made us,
       we are nothing.
     But that you strengthen us,
       we can do nothing.
     But that you love us,
       we can love no one.
     But that you show us,
       we can know nothing.
     But that you inspire us,
       we can believe no lasting truth.

       In these moments of sober reflection,
         in our heart of hearts,
         we know that the cold absence of deserving among us
         varies only by very small degree.

So it is,
    we long now, once more,
    for your harsh tenderness.
        We want the motives of our longings to be pure.
        We do not want our prayers to be pretense.
        Yet we can dig only so deep
            before the praying becomes too painful.
        Sort, then, we strongly beg,
            from among our provocations to pray
            and heed only those that are honest
            and true.
        Fill us with such grace
            that we might take advantage
            of this season of truth faced
            to renew our resolve to be faithful.

Is this too the acceptable time?
Is this too the day of our salvation?
Yes, Lord.
We believe it is.
Forgive our unbelief.

We pray in the name of Jesus Christ. Amen.

~~~~~~~

A Litany for the Close of Day on Maundy Thursday or Good Friday (51)

With a voice like lullaby and thunder,
    recreate the earth and sky,
    the moon and all stars,
    every living beast, bird, and swarming creature.
        Call forth from this night of dread
            healing for all things great and small.[2]
With breath like sparrow and hurricane,
    breathe again into these nostrils the breath of life.
        Call forth from this night of fear
            healing for all your people.
With a lonesome stride,
    stroll through the garden in the cool of this day
    and name again the shame of our longing to be God.
        Call forth from this night of dishonor
            the transgression of our way.

With the fumes of perdition,
    cry out in prophet tones.
        Call forth from this night of disgrace
          a vision of what is right.
With anthems clear,
    from the green fields near the edge of this city,
    for those with ears to hear,
    the angels are singing of peace on earth and goodwill toward all.
        Call forth from this night of reproach
          a longing to return to the promise of Bethlehem.
From every Christian pulpit in the land,
    the slow-tread story of Jesus rings out its bitter end.
        Call forth from this night of infamy
          for the story of Easter to begin.
In the name of the Christ who died.
    Amen.

A Pastoral Prayer for Maundy Thursday Night (52)

Lord God, we are your people.
We have come to worship you.
On this night,
    your worshiping people are filled with few words
    and many prayers:
        Prayers that come welling up
          from silent secret places deep within;
        Prayers that have more stark emotion
          than intelligible expression;
        Prayers that long,
          from the dark underside of being,
          for the light of your countenance.

Here, then, are our prayers
    whispered on earth in the quiet of this night
    that they will ring
    through the corridors of heaven
    with the wonder of disciples gathered
    for a ponderous meal:
        To those who have struggled and fallen,
          give courage to carry on.

> To those broken from some dark struggle,
>   give healing.
> To those who wait and pray for their struggle to end,
>   give hope.

On this night of comfort and cruelty,
    as we find a voice for prayer,
    we see we have more prayers yet welling up within us:
        Rid the world of tyranny, we pray,
            and call the tyrants to repent.
        Be with those who seek to take the high moral ground,
            and show them the direction of your moving.
        Be with those who, in this sin-soaked world, must find compromise,
            and give them the courage of forgiveness.
        Be with those who are persecuted for righteousness' sake,
            and give them the kingdom of heaven.
        Be with the peacemakers,
            and call them your sons and daughters.

Heal the sick.
Bind up the brokenhearted.
Give a warm place to the homeless.
Give food to the hungry.
Give courage to the fearful.
Make of us the body of Jesus Christ
    that we might be answers
    to the prayers we make in his name. Amen.

꙳꙳꙳꙳꙳꙳꙳

A Litany of Darkness and Light for the Dawn of Easter Day (53)

Lord God, out of the darkness of our lives
    and the darkness of this world,
    we come to the light of this new day.
        Hear our prayer
            and fill us with the hope and wonder of Easter.[3]
There is darkness
    beneath the cold sod of our places of burial.
        The Light shines in darkness,
            and darkness has not overcome it.[4]

With the conflicts in the world of our youth,
    with the conflicts in the homes of our birth,
    with the conflicts in the hearts of our growing,
    there are dark shadows
    cast along the paths
    of how we came to be who we are.
        The Light shines in darkness,
          and darkness has not overcome it.
With passions that have burned and secrets that are kept,
    we know the dark follies of youth
    and also the dark indiscretions of the age of knowing.
        The Light shines in darkness,
          and darkness has not overcome it.
With our homes today
    standing as the places of our hearts,
    we know there are dark corners that cannot be shown.
        The Light shines in darkness,
          and darkness has not overcome it.
With the story of the church
    soiled with petty bickering
    and brazen acts of injustice and immorality,
    we have morbid reason to hide.
        The Light shines in darkness,
          and darkness has not overcome it.
With the whole wide world on the brink of disaster
    and large parts of the world living with hunger and war,
    there is dark reason to fear that
    the dark side of the human spirit is sure to win.
        The Light shines in darkness,
          and darkness has not overcome it.
Our Easter prayers do not well
    from the depths of despair.
        Hear our prayer and accept our thanks
          for the hope and wonder of Easter's promise.

There is splendor and miracle in the life we have
    and in the life we share.
        Thy Light has come
          and the glory of the Lord is risen upon us.[5]
There is goodness and love
    in the nurturing people
    who have brought us thus far
    and made us who we are.

Thy Light has come
    and the glory of the Lord is risen upon us.
Our homes are places of warmth to family
    and hospitality to friends and to strangers.
        Thy Light has come
            and the glory of the Lord is risen upon us.
The church has proclaimed to us
    the goodness of God
    and faithfully been for us
    the body of Jesus Christ
    where, in those before us and in each other,
    we have known the living Spirit of God.
        Thy Light has come
            and the glory of the Lord is risen upon us.
The world we know is filled with beauty,
    and with bounty,
    and with people in whom there is great, great good.
        Thy Light has come
            and the glory of the Lord is risen upon us. Amen.

᳅᳅᳅᳅᳅᳅᳅

A Wedding Prayer for Jayne and Darren[6] (54)

With the sound of thunder and brook, O God,
    you speak across ages as countless as stars
    to concoct for a season this world and that.
With the breath of cyclone and sparrow,
    you blow into the nostrils of unnumbered generations
    to give life for a season to this creature and that.
With hands calloused and tender,
    you touch the thin sinew of mortals in time
    and show us each one in season by turn
    to love and be loved.
        Speak now to Jayne and Darren
            in the full glad laughter
            of this curious assemblage.
        Breathe now on Darren and Jayne
            in the bright frolic of strings
            making music of their choosing.[7]
        Touch now Jayne and Darren
            in the soft memory of magic,
                when their smallest fingers first brushed
                as if by chance.

From the deep edges of your speaking and breathing and touching
   in this playful and serious moment of ceremony,
   give Darren and Jayne new meaning
   to the linking of ancient words
   such as can be found in every known language.
     The words of which we speak
       are complex in nuance.
         They are words like these:

            I love you;
            I am sorry;
            I forgive;

            You are wrong;
            You are right;
            You are amazing;

            You seem sad;
            You seem happy;
            You seem ready to play;

            May I help?
            Will you help?
            Come, let us do this together;

            And, again, I love you;

            And again and at last,
              I love you.

With these words from every known language
   welled and drawn from the ancient truth of days
   and planted fresh in the secret places of these two hearts,
   we pray you will startle their considerable imaginations
   in a thousand million variations;

   and with these words given life,
   grant that Jayne and Darren
   shall be joined in marriage that is blessed
   and is a blessing
   to all these who for them have boundless love
   and who in them have shameless pride.

With bold confidence
   we ask these things
   in the name and spirit of Jesus Christ. Amen.

༅༅༅༅༅༅༅

A Wedding Prayer for Margaret and Brian[8] (55)

We are a curious mix, O God,
   gathered in from the high roads of many places,
   brought together
   in the love given Brian and Margaret.
      Here in these glad moments,
         the family of one
         is the family of all
         and the friends of one
         are the friends of all.

      Thank you, O God of love and kindness,
         for your imaginative providence
         that brings us to pray as one people
         on this day of your sure making.

We are wondrously made,
   created in your image, each one,
   knit together
   in the fragile strength of personhood.
      Here in this glad worship,
         love as ancient as days
         is as fresh as the morning
         and the love that created us
         is the love of this new founding.

      Thank you, O God of love and tenderness,
         for your imaginative providence
         that includes us in fashioning new places to live
         and in the construct of this brave new beginning.

We are the yield of much experience,
   united now in our joyful longing,
   met together
   in all our collective foolishness and wisdom.

Here in this glad praying
   we see in Margaret and Brian
   a love that is both strong and gentle
   born of the strong and gentle love
   given them and us in the being of Jesus.

      Thank you, O God of love and grace,
         for your imaginative providence
         that has brought love's tender touch
         to make these hearts cheerful
         and brought love's strong hand
         to heal when love's tenderness is bruised.

We make all our prayers in the name of Jesus Christ. Amen.

༄༄༄༄༄༄༄

A Prayer for Leila[9] (56)

Lord God,
   we are here stumbling over words
   to make of them prayers,
   as altogether mortal prayers
   can ever be prayers.
      Give us grace to imagine
         what our eyes cannot see
         and,
         by your Holy Spirit of Jesus Christ
         blowing fresh in this place,
         keep our imagining faithful.

Dispatch quickly, then, we pray,
   several of your most *thoughtful and sure*[10] heralds
   full of *good cheer and calm.*
      Have them open *quietly* the windows
         and make fresh the place prepared for Leila . . .
         prepared just for Leila . . .
         prepared for her
         from before the foundation of the earth.

Your faithful servant has just arrived
   and is, we are quite certain,
   attending matters of joyful greeting,
   first to one and then to the other,
   of those whom she has loved
   and whose memory she savored long.
Soon, very soon,
   when the greeting is done,
   she will wish to claim her place of *quiet rest*.
It is,
   we are quite sure,
   a place of *character*
   and hospitality
   where family is given glad welcome
   and conversation has a bright, reflective,
   and easy flow.

Then, O loving God,
   by whose voice worlds are made,
   by whose breath we breathe,
   and in whose Word we hope,
   with your servant safe at home,
   dispatch quickly to this place
   a fresh new whisper and spirit
   from the ancient truth of days.
      Speak tenderly to these broken hearts.
      Hold them in gentle strength
         until the day of their mending.
      Round for them
         the edges of memory
         that Leila's mantle now cast
         might bring *affectionate comfort*
         to those who wear it:
            Devoted children and the mates of their bringing;
            Grandchildren of their adding;
            Great-grandchildren lately arriving;
            Grateful students with stories yet telling.

   Give grace to *us* all, O loving God,
      that in these who now wear Leila's cloak,
      we might see the signs of your kingdom
      that in her we saw so clearly.

In ways strange for us to hear and say,
    as thousands before us have strangely prayed,
    we too are glad that for Leila pain is ended
    and she has entered the life of your knowing.
Yet now,
    for the day of this living,
    we thank you for signs of hope:
        Family yet gathering;
        Church yet praying;
        Children yet laughing.

In the name and hope of Christ we pray. Amen.

A Prayer for Al[11] (57)

Lord God,
    we have come to believe deeply
    that you brought again from the dead
    our Lord Jesus Christ.
Because that is so,
    we've come also to believe
    that through him,
    long before time,
    as the likes of us can ever know time,
    you prepared a place for Al Smith;

    and we've come to believe
    that long, long after time,
    as the likes of us can now know time,
    you'll keep right on preparing that place just for Al Smith.

        You've given us no clear picture
            of exactly what that place is like,
                but you've put some ideas of it in our minds,
                and in those ideas we take great comfort.
        When we think of it,
            to the eyes of our mind and heart,
            the place prepared for Al Smith
            looks out over *mountains and hills*[12]
            purple in the fresh dampness of morning light
            and *deep soft green* in the evening shade.

The place for Al is a place of *warm welcome and easy laughter*
for friends and creatures of every sort to gather
and for the growing of all manner of familiar things.
It has, we are sure, *a shed to one side*
in which is parked a long yellow school bus,
useful in the hauling of children who behave themselves—
but not too much.
We know their laughter is playful and happy.

Lord God,
Al has labored long and hard
with this dread disease that ate away at nearly all of his body parts.
Put now his strong spirit
in a strong being
of the sort made new.
Give him glad reunion
with those whom he loved.
Settle him at last
in the place prepared for him,
there to wait long years that will seem short
for the others whom he loved.

Then, Lord God,
with Al all settled and satisfied,
come quickly to this place
and visit with solace these hearts heavy with grief.
Thelma and Shirley are tired to the marrow of their bone
and their spirits are struck hard and low.
What sweetness there is in knowing pain has ended
is made salty with the tears of deep sorrow.
Give them rest in the certainty
that they did well
in making Al's leave as easy
as it could possibly have been.
Bathe their wounds with the balm of your kindness.
Bind their wounds with the cloth of your grace.
Heal their wounds slowly
and from the inside out
so there will be no festering behind the scars.

Bless also those who by birth
or by marriage
or by devotion
are family.

Bless them in ties that bind beyond death's breaking,
    and fill them with the hope of this and every new day.
Bless this community of faith at home in these mountains and hills
    spread east now to near the ocean's mighty shore.
Bless all of your servants near and afar,
    whose gentle touch is your gentle touch,
    whose kind word is your kind word,
    and whose strong presence is your strong presence.

Fill us with such faith in Jesus Christ
    that we might have confidence
    in the well-being of the ones we must release to your care.
Make holy this small piece of your good earth
    into which we place the body of Al Smith
    that it will be a sacred place to come and remember;
    but give us all eyes to see beyond this place
    to a house not made with hands;
    then hold us all in your hands
    while we live the fullness of this
    and all our days.

      We pray in the strong name of Jesus Christ,
        our risen Savior,
        in whom we place our hope. Amen.

A Prayer for Walk[13] (58)

Lord, our God,
    how very excellent is your name in all the earth.
      We come to this prayer with a complex mixture of emotions:

      We are here, most of us,
        sure in the answers we have found or been given;
        yet uneasy with the questions that go wanting.

      We are grateful for the gift of life;
        yet perplexed that this life ended as it did.

      Our hearts are at peace in what was done to make Walk better;
        yet restless in what could not be done.

Today we are relieved that, for Walk, illness has ended;
yet we wish there had been more time for a miracle.

This holy hour with family and close, close friends finds us
secure in the ties that bind our hearts together,
yet sad that this tie is now broken for a season.

We dare to speak this prayer just now
strangely satisfied in dreams that have been fulfilled;
yet empty because of plans that must go unfinished.

We pray
taking comfort in what we believe,
yet grieving without shame because of this great, great loss.

In the midst of all this complexity,
we shall speak no bumbling words
explaining to you our brave understanding
of this sad thing that has happened.
We have no such understanding.

We pray rather just this:
that you will make sacred the memory of Walk Jones;
that you will bless the legacy of buildings short and tall built,
every one of them,
as testimony to blending his creation
with your creation;
bless also the legacy of the institutions he
nurtured,
every one of them to join his healing
with your healing;
above all,
bless the legacy of the family he leaves,
so good,
every one of them
molded to fit their being
to your holy image.
Bless Sissy, left lonely.
Bless the children, all five of them,
now no longer at all children
but feeling just now so very small.

> Bless grandchildren and the hope they have brought
>   and yet promise to bring.
> Bless friends left wondering what to do.
> Bless the church.
> Oh, yes, bless the church.
> Call forth quickly the many needed
>   to fill Walk's dreams
>   of the church's full faithfulness.

Already you have made holy this piece of good earth
    as a place of sacred rest;
    but help us to see beyond this holy ground
    to a house not made with hands,
    eternal in the heavens.
        We're quite sure Walk will be struck with awe at your architecture.

We pray in the name of Jesus Christ,
    risen and living,
    in whom these prayers
    and our sure hope are possible. Amen.

☙☙☙☙☙☙☙

A Prayer for Gary[14] (59)

Lord God,
    the feelings here are many, and
    the feelings here are varied.
O Lord God,
    the feelings here run together in such collision
    we can scarcely separate them
    or know at all what to do with them.
The prayers are too many for us to find words for them all.
In fact,
    for our deepest prayers we don't have words
    and would gladly sit with our heads bowed
    in utter silence,
    trusting that you will hear what we cannot speak.

And yet, O God,
    there are some prayers which we can,
    if we dare,
    stumble through
    and trust you to keep us from falling.

There are in this house of worship today
those who are angry.
Be with us, Lord, and hear our anger
that its red-hot heat may be cooled
and its strength used
not to destroy
but to build.
There are those in this house of worship today
who are bitter.
There is no power
that should make the bitterness sweet;
but by your power, O God,
turn our bitterness to fashion resolve
to make of this a safer place to live.
There are some here
who are frightened.
Give calm, O God,
that helps us see the promise of your Spirit.
There are some here
who have overwhelming feelings of hopelessness.
Show to them the hope born in Jesus Christ,
which can change despair into assurance.
All who are here today
are filled with grief;
in that we are the same
and differ only by degree.
Bring healing, O God,
but not too quickly,
lest the pain of all be covered
with hope that is shallow.
Give the gift of time
to these who wait on your Holy Spirit,
and by your Holy Spirit
working in the lives of all of these
bring comfort to those who grieve most.

Accept our thanks, O God,
for the gift of the life of Gary Taylor.
We are grateful for all that in him
was good and kind and faithful.

Accept our thanks, O God,
for your promise to him that is now fulfilled.

We are grateful for the peace he now experiences
and the understanding he now enjoys.

Accept our thanks, O God,
for the gift of memory
that allows those who loved him so dearly
to reflect on the joy of having known and loved him.
We are grateful for his good influence
that lives on in those who grieve.

Be especially with Kathy and Alison and Blake.
Support them.
Sustain them.
Help them to be open
to those who by surrounding them in their own love
surround them also in your love.
Be also with [here were named other members of his family].
The grief of family is so very, very deep and real.
Give them grace, O God,
not so much to make sense of this thing
which makes no sense,
but in order that they may lean on you and each other.
Be strongly with all these strong friends,
each of whom is filled with stories to tell
of love and devotion to Gary.

Bless this city, O God,
and those who labor to make it safe.
Bring upon this city
some power as strong as a refiner's fire,
not to destroy
but to make clean and new
both the desperate
and the desperately mean.
Bring quickly the day
when senseless death shall be no more
and our questions will no more go unanswered.

We pray in the name of Jesus Christ. Amen.

۞۞۞۞۞۞۞

A Prayer for Mary Elizabeth[15] (60)

Eternal God:
    By one way of our thinking,
        you created us from the dust of the earth
        and breathed into our nostrils the breath of life.
    By another way of our thinking,
        you intricately knit us together in our mother's womb.
            We do most sincerely thank you for the gift of life
                and, especially today,
                we thank you for the gift of the life of
                Mary Elizabeth Calhoun.

Jesus, born of a young woman named Mary and the power of God:
    At a time,
        you lived among us to love and be loved,
        you touched and healed,
        you died and live,
        that even in death
        we fear no evil
        and trust your strength
        to make life stronger than death.
            We do most sincerely thank you for the gift of faith
                and, especially today,
                we thank you for the gift of the faith
                given to Mary Elizabeth Calhoun
                by which she has now found rest and understanding.

Holy Spirit, presence of God blowing among us:
    By your movement,
        generations have found strength and courage
        to move into the uncertain future
        to face life with hope that is more than eyes can see.
            We do most sincerely thank you for the gift of presence,
                and especially we thank you for the gift of your presence
                in all these who loved Mary Elizabeth,
                cherish strong memories,
                and grieve deeply her death.
                    Bless her left-lonesome husband;
                    Bless her faithful daughter;
                    Bless her heartbroken grandchildren;

Bless all in her family
and among her friends
who wait some word of meaning
and who fear the uncertainty of living.

Heal these wounds, we pray,
but not too quickly,
that in time
they heal from the inside out
to leave scars
but no disease to cripple.

We thank you, O God,
for the gift of faithfulness
and especially for the gift of faithfulness
that wound its way through Mary Elizabeth's strong character
and leaves now a legacy to be savored.

Merciful God,
this life is so uncertain.
Even a long life
is but a handful of days
weighed against the ages.
We are grateful for Mary Elizabeth's long life
and that, for her, death was painless.
Even so,
give us grace to number our days
not in morbid foreboding
but in the joy of counting each moment
and filling each moment with purpose and value
and gladness and laughter
and caring and kindness
and gentleness and thoughtfulness
and standing for what is right and good.
There is so little time,
so help us to cherish the gift
that comes on the wings of each new day.

Now, God,
guard and protect all of these your servants
and especially protect those who in the coming days,

weeks, months, and years
will give voice and hand
to your grace in the lives of these who grieve.

We pray in the name of Jesus Christ. Amen.

❧❧❧❧❧❧❧

A Funeral Prayer[16] (61)

Lord God, hear us as we pray.
You are the God of time
    and the God of eternity.
Your realm is here,
    yet more than here.
You are the God of life as we savor it
    and the God of life that is beyond our imagining.
You have made yourself known
    to probing minds and longing hearts,
    yet you remain an unfathomable mystery
    to intrigue and inspire those who will
    ever to reach to your beckoning.

We pause just now
    to thank you for the gift of the life
    of your servant, (Name),
    whose path these gathered were privileged to cross.
We are especially grateful for (Gifts of the deceased).
Strengthen among these who grieve
    the twin gifts of memory and hope
    that this life so rich in (Attributes of the deceased)
    may inspire and challenge for yet a season and more.
Do not remove, we pray, this sadness.
To do so may render shallow the devotion by which these gather.
Yet we do pray that this sadness may be surrounded
    with the hope of life yet to live,
    and dreams yet to dream,
    and adventures yet to take
    in this life and the next.

We are grateful that for (Name), death is ended
and pain is past
and (he or she) is now at rest.

All of these prayers are made in the name of Jesus Christ. Amen.

❧❧❧❧❧❧❧

A Service of Prayer for the Night of September 11, 2001[17] (62)
The Creation: Genesis 1:1–4a

God of mercy and of grace,
you created this beautiful world,
filled it with light,
and declared it good;

and yet at the end of this hard day
we are stumbling in darkness so deep
no human eye can penetrate.
We cannot see beyond the raw unspeakable ugliness
of this dismal moment.
Cold, still death has come in the heat of insane rage
unleashed on the innocents.
Mortals created in your image
have done these horrible acts,
and we are left with nothing but ashes
and perplexity
and anger
and fear
and deep sadness,
and questions . . . endless questions . . .
all of that
and faith that trembles in its hunger for righteousness.

Come, Spirit of God.
Move again across this dark void
and bring new light . . .
bring new light . . .
bring especially the light of your direction
for those mortals among us
faced with endless and wrenching decisions.

We pray in the name of Jesus Christ, the light of the world. Amen.

The Fall: Genesis 3:1–10

Merciful God,
   many of our sisters and brothers in this land of ours
   have witnessed and had seared on the eye of memory
   the horror of what it means in the extreme
   to wish to be like God.
      All of us have seen the pictures:
         smoke billowing,
         people running,
         wreckage scattered,
         ambulances screeching,
         fire engines blaring,
         human bodies in free fall.

   We all, every one,
      can be seen in the cool of this night
      trying to cover the shame of our nakedness.
   There is no innocence.
   You see us all,
      every one,
      just as we are;

      and yet,
      for some,
      for a very few, we deeply pray,
      the loss of innocence is beyond imagining.

         Who are these who conceived such plans?
         Who are these who execute?
         What are their names?
         Bring justice . . . bring your justice:
            expose them,
            name them,
            curse them;

         and then,
         by some strange twist of mercy,
         make them whole again.

      Redeem us all and make us whole again.

      We pray in the name of the Redeemer. Amen.

The Promise: Genesis 12:1–4

Merciful God,
    from the barren womb of Sarah,
    a womb more barren than any known desert,
    you brought forth the only final hope we know to trust.
        Move across this now barren land
            and especially its places parched
            by fireballs of human habitation,
            driven from the sky by mad men,
            to crash and kill and maim and sicken with grief.

Call us once more.
Call *us.*
We are your newly chosen people.
Call us to take the first brave and faithful steps
    from this bleak time and barren place
    into the sure hope of your leading.
Give us courage born of faith
    to take those steps
    and then to lead others with us
    to the sanity of your promise.
Heal the deepest wounds
    of those who grieve most
    that, in time,
    we may bravely pray your healing
    for those whose rage and madness
    caused this pervasive pain.
        From the promise given to Abraham and Sarah
            we firmly believe,
            when the time was right,
            you gave us Jesus of Nazareth,
            in whose name we pray this night. Amen.

The Lament: Psalm 22 (selected verses)

Merciful God,
    we do not dare put ourselves in league with Jesus.
        Even on the days of our most sincere following,
            we have died for no one's sin
            as Jesus died for the sins of us all.
        Yet and so,
            we are deeply grateful that he dared to put himself
            in league with us
            and taught us from the cross
            that it is right and good
            to call your hand
            when we feel forsaken.

            Where were you when these deeds were planned?
            Where were you when the tickets were bought?
            Where were you when the planes were commandeered?
            Where were you when the people were going to work . . .
                just going to work . . .
                just taking trips . . .
                just tending matters of the day?
                    Had you no word to say?
                    Had you no great hand to wave?
                    Had you no different breath to blow?

Yet we do strangely believe you are God.
We more strangely believe also you were there
    when the planes were crashed:
    there to hold gently the dying,
    and there to be the first to grieve,
    and here to be present to bind these broken hearts.

        We will reverently speak your holy name in the congregation.
        We will faithfully praise you even as we dare to question you.

In the name of the one who also said,

        "My God, my God, why have you forsaken me?" Amen.

The Help: Psalm 90 (selected verses)

(The prayer was the hymn "Our God, Our Help in Ages Past," set to the tune of ST. ANNE.)

The Prophecy: Isaiah 11:1–9

Merciful God,
  we have come to believe to the marrow of our bone
  that Jesus of Nazareth is the root from the stump of Jesse,
  who judges not from what he sees and hears
  but by the spirit of knowledge and the fear of the Lord.

  Come, Lord Jesus, come quickly.
  We can only judge by what we see and what we hear.
  We need wise counsel.
  Our leaders need judgment that is greater
    than any mortal can ever have.
  Speak, Holy Spirit of Jesus Christ.
  Speak to rulers of this earth
    and especially to our president
    and to all who advise him.

  Remove all motive for political posturing.
  Bring down the vengeance that belongs to you
    and to you alone.
  Heap your wrath on the heads of the guilty
    that the rulers of this world
    be not tempted to embrace the sin of terror
    and may thus, instead,
    concentrate more on healing
    than on getting even . . .

    more on peace
    than on war . . .

    more on hope
    than on despair.

And, O Lord our God,
    keep the church dreaming of a peaceable kingdom.

    We pray in the name of the Prince of peace. Amen.

The Stillness: Psalm 46 and Psalm 23

(The prayer was the hymn "The Lord's My Shepherd, I'll Not Want," set to the tune of CRIMOND.)

The Fulfillment: Luke 2:8–14

Merciful God,
    for those keeping watch in the fields this night,
    the only hymn they are apt to hear from the angels
    is a funeral dirge;

    and yet in this place
    we have yet the memory of the other night
    when the angels sang a different song . . .

    a song of peace and goodwill.

      With the light of that memory,
        give us vision to see through this present darkness.

We pray in the name of the one in whom there was no darkness. Amen.

The Blessing: Matthew 5:1–16

How strange it is, O merciful God,
    to think of ourselves as among the blessed
    as Jesus named the blessed.
      The only blessing we feel
        is that we were not in harm's way
        on this harm-filled day.

And yet,
>> we are among the poor in spirit
>> or long to be;
>> we are without a doubt
>> among those who mourn evil;
>> we are the meek or long to be;
>> those who hunger for righteousness
>> or long to hunger for righteousness;
>> we are the merciful or wish to be;
>> the pure in heart or long to be;
>> the peacemakers, yes we long to be;
>> and maybe even the persecuted for righteousness' sake.

> We are, then, among the blessed.

You name us salt of the earth and light of the world.
Give us the grace of Jesus Christ
> that we might be savor in these bitter days
> and that we might be light to shine in these dark nights.

> We pray in the name of the One who blessed and named us. Amen.

The Comfort: Romans 8 (selected verses)

Lord God,
>> make ready the place prepared for those who have died;
>> bind the wounds of those who are injured;
>> mend in time the broken hearts;
>> direct toward healing the rage of the very, very angry;
>> guide the perplexed;
>> dry these tears;
>> protect those who are placed now in war's alarm;
>> bless those who sit and wait for those placed in war's alarm; and
>> from the horror of what has happened to us,
>> give us new eyes to see the fear of those who live daily
>> in the reach of senseless terror;

>> then fill us with the sure belief
>> that there is no terror that has or ever shall

separate us from the love of God
in Jesus Christ our Lord,
in whose name we pray. Amen.

The Hope: John 14:25–27 and Revelation 21:1–4

(The prayer was the hymn "A Mighty Fortress Is Our God," set to the tune of
EIN' FESTE BURG.)

ᘓᘓᘓᘓᘓᘓ

A Prayer for a Search Committee[18] (63)

God of mercy and of grace,
 you have spoken in voices loud and voices small.
  Listen now,
   not to the deserving of our voices,
   but to the yearning of our hearts.
God of truth and of grace,
 by the strength of your voice the earth gives life.
  Listen now,
   not so much to the strength of our demands
   as to the passion of our longings.
God of wisdom and of grace,
 by the Spirit of Christ your Word lives in this
 unlikely assembly of your servants
 brought together for the purpose
 of a particular searching after your will.
  Listen now,
   not to the logic of our cases argued,
   but to the hope of our sure belief
   that you have chosen to listen . . .
   to listen very, very carefully.

There is a person,
 we are quite sure,
 a particular person
 in whose being you laugh with delight
 and in whose gifts you take shameless pride;
 a person chosen and known

before she or he was knit together for the purpose;
a person shaped in time
to be dean of this blessed place of promise and hope.

    By the testimony of those before us
        and by our own sure conviction,
        we strangely believe you strangely see
        these grand and wonderful things.
    By that same testimony and conviction,
        we are quite certain you also know,
        on this glad day,
        we don't have a clue.

Be patient with us, we piously pray,
    as we search out your will in this matter of consequence;
    but do not,
    we strongly pray,
    be so patient with us that you should forget
    why you called us to this task.

For now,
    we pray you will bless this person
    of your delight and shameless pride,
    unknown to us but known to you;
    and bless also this curious mix of pilgrims
    in our slow-tread race
    down the path of your making
    that will lead us in season
    to be the voice of your calling.

    We pray in the name of Jesus Christ. Amen.

⚬⚬⚬⚬⚬⚬

A Prayer for the Campbell Scholars at the Start of Day[19] (64)

Lord God of time,
    remember no more the evil of days long and recently gone,
    but help us never to forget;
    remember well the good of days long and recently gone,
    and help us in it all
    to be filled with hope in your presence and in your coming.

Lord God of time,
    weep deeply at the great pain of this day,
    and give healing ointment for us to apply;
    laugh robustly at the gladness of this day,
    and help us in it all
    to be filled with hope in your presence and in your coming.

Lord God of time,
    dread intensely the anguish of tomorrow's scheme,
    and show us how to turn the tide of greed;
    anticipate eagerly the delight of tomorrow's promise,
    and help us in it all
    to be filled with hope in your presence and in your certain coming.

Lord God of eternity,
    as you most surely imagined this remarkable assembly,
    inspire in us on this remarkable day
    such imagination that we shall be
    amazed
    and astounded
    by the vision given in what we hunger and thirst to see.
      We long to see clearly
        a time in time and beyond
        when, in the promised reign of God,
        all the children will laugh and play,
        and all the young will dream and plan,
        and all the grown-ups will burst with contentment,
        and all the old will sigh deeply in the wisdom of our years.
      Where vision on this day fails,
        fill us with trust in the risen Christ,
        in whose name we pray. Amen.

෧෧෧෧෧෧෧

Another Prayer for the Campbell Scholars at the Start of Day (65)

God who is far,
    so far there is no yearning eye can see . . .
    so far there is no praying voice can reach . . .
    so far there is no longing arm can touch . . .

God who is near,
> so near there is no leaf of color nor person you do not behold in delight . . .
> so near there is no laughing creature nor mortal you do not heed in joy . . .
> so near there is no stirring wind nor human spirit you do not feel
>> in gladness,

> listen carefully, we pray,
> listen in all of your distance,
> listen more in all of your presence.

> We're praying for a vision . . .
>> not a fantasy . . .
>> not an illusion . . .
>> not an invention, but a vision:

>> A promised place where children do not throw stones;
>> A promised place where soldiers do not shoot children;
>> A promised place where tyrants sit in dark silence;
>> A promised place where airplanes do not fall from the sky;
>> A promised place where disease does not destroy;
>> A promised place where sons and fathers are not taken in the night;
>> A promised place where daughters and mothers walk in safety;[20]
>> A promised place where women and men stand side by side;
>> A promised place where the poor are seated at the banquet;
>> A promised place where the rich learn dignity from the poor;
>> A promised place where truth is spoken;
>> A promised place where there is no mourning,
>>> nor crying,
>>> nor pain,
>>> nor despair,[21]
>>> anymore
>>> for the former things shall have passed away.

Then,
> like a mother comforting her child,
> wipe away every tear from their eye and ours;
> and with this vision of divine promise,
> give us grace to live in faithfulness
> and hope
> as we face the tasks that are before us this day.

We pray in the name of Jesus Christ, our risen Lord. Amen.

A Prayer of Dedication for Confirmands (66)

Lord God,
    you spoke and worlds came to be,
    in Jesus Christ your Word became flesh to dwell among us,
    then your Spirit blew across a curious lot
    and you named us the church.
We have now,
    in your odd providence,
    added the names of these known already to you
    to be among those who are also the church.
Place your benediction upon these your inquiring servants
    and upon the church they join.
        Make of their joys in the faith a celebration.
        Make of their questions in the faith a challenge.
        Make of their confidence in the faith a gladness.
        Make of their pilgrimage in the faith a growing.
        Make of their friends in the church a community.
        Make of their elders in the faith worthy examples.
We make all of our prayers in the name of Jesus Christ. Amen.

A Prayer for Billie[22] (67)

God of life and of hope,
God of tears and of good cheer,
God present in things fearfully real
    and in things playfully dreamed,
    this prayer is for your faithful servant, Billie:

    Bless Billie for a while yet,
        at least for a short while,
        with the good gift of forgetfulness,
        that the sounds of crashing metal and breaking glass
        be lost until a time of healing
        and the sight of a curious crowd and emergency angels
        not be recalled until a season of gratitude.

Bless her also for a short while,
   for not more than a short while,
   with the good gift of fanciful vision
   of dying once with no fear
   and of dying once again with no qualm
   and of clinging yet to the ship's strong mast in the raging storm
   and of children playing at a grand and sumptuous wedding feast.
     Keep all such dreams alive
      until the day of her returning
      to cling to sure and real faith
      in the midst of every strong and real storm
      and to dance once more in the joy of secure and real love.

Then,
   after a long, long, long time, we strongly pray,
   at the time of your right choosing,
   without fear or qualm,
   bring her safely to the place beyond place
   where even her best dreams from now
   will surely lack luster.
     We pray in the name of Jesus Christ. Amen.

Chapter 5

Prayers of Exiles Praying outside the Camp

Mighty God,
　　Creator of all that is,
　　of all that has been, and
　　of all that ever shall be,
　　heed now the prayers of your people
　　come from many places of understanding and belief
　　to pray with one voice to one holy God
　　known by many names.

　　　We are an enlightened people
　　　　who have trouble thinking of you
　　　　sitting on a throne of gold
　　　　and served by winged creatures
　　　　as you point this way and that,
　　　　making decrees for this and the other.
　　　It is hard for us to think of you creating
　　　　robins and whales and stars and people
　　　　by some strong word that echos across eons,
　　　　or by some hot breath that blows across ages,
　　　　or by some powerful wave of hand that reaches across infinity.
　　　　　Yet,
　　　　　　we have come to believe,
　　　　　　sometimes eagerly
　　　　　　and sometimes reluctantly,
　　　　　　that you create and rule this beautiful world,
　　　　　　gone mad for a long season, and
　　　　　　that you rule this nation

that some days pays you no heed
even when it calls us to give thanks.
We do give thanks.
To the marrow of our bone,
   we give thanks.

Gentle, strong God of these who strangely pray together . . .
God of our parents and of our children yet unborn,
   we have heard of you
   and of how you speak in many voices
   and of how you healed our diseases
   and of how you cured our warring madness.
      We have come curiously to believe
         that you shall over many days redeem this world,
         gone mad for a long season, and
         that you will call the hand of this nation
         even when this nation calls us to give thanks.
      We do give thanks.
      To the marrow of our bone,
         we give thanks.

Spirit of truth,
   you have come to us in our variety of custom and practice;
   come to us again
   that we might feel and hear your crisp movement,
   blowing as typhoon and sparrow's breath,
   to change as little as one pesky habit
   or as much and more as the fortunes of many greedy nations.
      We have come deeply to believe
         that some sure day we shall all understand
         this beautiful world,
         gone mad for a long season, and
         that the future of this nation
         is in your hands,
         even as it calls us to give thanks.
      We do give thanks.
      To the marrow of our bone,
         we give thanks

We are restless and the world is restless.
We have seen the promise of peace.
We grieve and the world grieves.
We have seen the promise of life.

We are ill and the world is ill.
We have seen the promise of health.
We are afraid and the world is afraid.
We have seen the promise of kindness.
We are wrong and the world is wrong.
We have seen the promise of forgiveness.
We are thankful.
To the marrow of our bone,
    we are thankful.
        Amen.

᠍᠍᠍᠍᠍᠍᠍᠍᠍᠍᠍᠍᠍᠍᠍

A Prayer for the Memphis City Commission (69)

O God and Source of all authority
    and of everything right and good,
    as far away as far
    yet as near as air,
    we are not so cavalier as to think by our governance
    we could conjure your presence.
        You will be where you choose to be,
            and we, most of us,
            believe you choose already to be here
            in all of your fearsome regard
            for the way of your mortals.

We pray, then,
    O God of all that is right and good,
    that you will watch carefully
    and listen intensely
    as these servants of the people
    come now as one body
    to serve the people.
        Use these men and women, we pray,
            to break down the walls of hostility that yet separate this city,
            to bind the wounds that yet fester in this city, and
            to nurture the good that yet flows naturally in this city.

    Where no choice can be for the well-being of all,
        give this council grace
        to make the better choice
        and the will to make amends with fidelity.

Where choices are between conflicting ideals strongly held,
   give members of this council grace
   to see with each other's eyes
   and the conviction to vote with courage that is kind.
When choices have been made,
   give the members of this council satisfaction in faithfulness,
   or the will to make change when faithfulness has failed,
   and courage to believe you have heard this prayer.

We pray in the Spirit of the one God
   who has helped this city in ages past
   and, we tremble to believe,
   is the hope of this city for years to come. Amen.

❧❧❧❧❧❧❧

A Prayer from the Balcony of the Loraine Motel[1] (70)

Lord God,
   we have made of this pain-filled place
   an altar for reverence.
Where once rang out
   the din of violence
   to silence the dreamer,
   we stand now
   in his memory
   to dream his dream
   and to pledge ourselves again
   to live his vision.
Shelter the memory of this people
   from the danger of forgetfulness,
   that we might learn from Dr. Martin Luther King Jr.
   and those who marched with him
   to long for all your children
   to be free from strife and poverty.
Protect the moments of this people
   from cowardice and complacency
   that we might take our places
   among those who stand for truth
   and together
   yet build here,
   in memory of Dr. King,
   a city set on a hill

where those who will can see
all your children
working
and playing
together.
Guard the hope of this people
from crippling fear and faithless doubt
that we may dare to dream the dream
of those who long for peace
and of those who touch with love
the lives of children.

Lord God,
among this people
gathered for the moment as one,
you are known by many names.
Together we name you God of hope
and together we pray in that glad name. Amen.

⌁⌁⌁⌁⌁⌁⌁

A Prayer for the Memphis Interfaith Association[2] (71)

Merciful God,
we do not ask
that you make of this city
the promised land;
and yet,
we have heard the cries of your people,
we have heard the whispers of their sighs,
and we have heard the thunder of their deafening silence.
When we reported their anguish to your attentive ear
we heard again your command
to face down the forces of every known Pharaoh.
From every crevice and hill of this city
we have demanded and yet demand
that your people be let go
from the bondage of poverty and ignorance.
Whether the bondage be
of the vestige of slavery,
of the wound of needles,
of the callus of indifference,
or the oppression of greed,

we have reported and here report again
that the God who is
commands that the people be set free.
No.
Do not make this city the promised land.
Rather, make it
an oasis in the desert,
a place of renewal
along the way to freedom.

Bless those in whom you inspired this dream.
Bless those by whom the dream is being fulfilled.
Bless these by whom the dream now flows.

Inspire, we pray, yet new and bigger dreams
and when vision grows dim
and hope seems distant,
move again among us with your holy presence.
Like a mysterious visitor at the Jabbock,
send an angel
or a mortal
or come your mighty self
to wrestle all night if need be
with those who rest their heads on this stone,
and give them grace not to turn you loose
until you have blessed them
along the way
to take the next brave steps
in their pilgrimage to your promise.

We make this prayer as sons and daughters of Abraham and Sarah,
every one,
and as brothers and sisters of Jesus, many.
Amen.

❦❦❦❦❦❦❦

A Prayer for the NAACP Gala[3] (72)

Eternal God,
Creator of all time and place,
visit just now this glad moment and festive hall
that you might be present

to hear the voice of our thanksgiving
and to bless this coming together
in the celebration
and hope
of freedom.
Accept our thanks, O God,
for those who have gone before
and for those not here
by whose conviction and toil
many dividing walls of hostility
have crumbled to dust.
And yet, O God,
there are walls yet remaining
that divide your people
one from the other:
not as many walls of the street
or walls of the yard
but walls of the heart
and walls of the mind.
They are walls more subtle than the others.
They are walls harder to knock down
and longer to go around.

Accept, then, our thanks
for all your faithful servants
yet in the vanguard of goodwill
by whose conviction and toil
remaining walls that divide
will someday crumble and fall.
Bless this food
and bless this occasion
that both will nourish and sustain
those in this hall
in whom truth marches on. Amen.

❧❧❧❧❧❧❧

Prayer for the Naturalization of New Citizens (73)

God of many names,
God of justice and of peace,

God of now and of always,
  look today with mercy upon these your people
  bowed now before the God in whom we trust,
  as our coins boldly attest.
Lord God,
  though our understanding of you may vary,
  our prayer in this place
  is that by your Spirit moving among us
  the spoken prayer of this one
  will become strangely the prayer of all
  and that the prayer of all
  will more strangely still
  be the prayer of each one.
We pray also, O God,
  that the secret prayers which here go unspoken
  will reach an attentive ear.

  Accept our thanks
    for the United States of America and
    for all that in her is yet true and just and free.
  Give to each of us, we pray,
    the desire to protect her from evil
    and to mend her every
    flaw.

  Accept our thanks also, O God,
    for the brave men and women and their children
    who, though born on foreign shores,
    have stood thus before
    and pledged their allegiance to this nation.
  Be now with these
    who come to stand in their shadows
    to take a place in this land of the free
    and this home of the brave
    or for those who long to be.
      Give purity of heart and clarity of vision.
      Protect and guide.
      Inspire and encourage.

  Give to the nation grace to welcome.
  Bless our president and all who govern.

Bless and inspire all who are governed
    that the dream of government of the people,
    by the people,
    for the people
    might play in the hearts of us all. Amen.

⧽⧽⧽⧽⧽⧽⧽

A Prayer for District Attorney General Gibbons[4] (74)

God whose word is truth
    and whose truth is final:
        We pray now for your servant
           as we charge him
           to divide truth among us.

God whose will is justice
    and whose justice shall abound:
        We pray now for your servant
           as we charge him
           to occasion justice among us.

God whose way is peace on earth
    and whose peace shall at last be known:
        We pray for your servant
           as we charge him
           to engender peace among us.

God whose essence is grace
    and whose grace has the character of mercy:
        We pray for your servant
           as we charge him
           to know when mercy must abound.

    When the shouts all about him
        are shrill and conflicted,
        speak to him in a still, small voice of calm.

    When there is no sound about him
        save the sound of lonely silence,
        speak to him in the memory of many brave voices.

When his work is put to rest,
 give to him the laughter of family
 and the knowledge of a job faithfully done. Amen.

⌘⌘⌘⌘⌘⌘⌘

A Prayer for the Memphis Symphony League (75)

Lord God,
 we are blessed and grateful
 to live among people
 who join you in particular ways
 to compose that which is lovely,
 to conceive that which inspires, and
 to re-create that which kindles within us
 things noble and kind and thoughtful.

 Bless all artists in this hall, we pray,
  and those who gather here to support them.
 Bless this food
  and our time about these tables.
 Bless those who prepare
  and those who serve this feast.

We pray in the name of the One who is holy
 and who creates all things beautiful. Amen.

⌘⌘⌘⌘⌘⌘⌘

A Prayer for Relay for Life[5] (76)

God of grace and God of glory,
 you are known to us by many names.
  Our prayer tonight is to the One who is the great Healer.

 These faithful servants,
  come from many faiths and many places
  to this place,
  are here for one task
  with many faces.

Use these people and this event
to bring healing:

Healing to those who have struggled long with disease;
Healing to those whose struggle has just begun;
Healing to those who are filled with hope;
Healing to those who are deeply discouraged;
Healing to those who faithfully stand near to serve;
Healing for those who labor daily in the healing arts; and
Healing to those who grieve.

Keep safe all those who walk this long night through, we pray,
and fill them with good cheer in the course of their noble task. Amen.

Notes

INTRODUCTION

1. Walter Brueggemann, *Cadences of Home: Preaching among Exiles* (Louisville, Ky.: Westminster John Knox, 1997), 2.

2. The quote is a paraphrase from Joshua 24:15.

3. See Luke 4:16–21.

4. Brueggemann, *Cadences of Home*, 3.

CHAPTER 2: PASTORAL PRAYERS
FOR EXILES AT WORSHIP ON THE LORD'S DAY

1. The given name of an infant who had been baptized earlier in the service.

2. This portion of the prayer may be used as a litany, with the congregation praying the words that are printed in italic.

3. A second major hurricane of the season had just left unprecedented floodwaters in eastern North Carolina.

4. George W. Bush had just been sworn in as president after a famously less than decisive election.

5. This portion of the prayer may be used as a litany, with the congregation praying the words that are printed in italic.

6. Bishop Jesse Williams, pastor of Mt. Zion Holiness Church, an African American congregation in New Bern, North Carolina, was preaching at the First Presbyterian Church of that city in observance of the Martin Luther King holiday.

7. At the time this prayer was written, the news was filled with reports of yet another school shooting at which there had been much loss of life.

8. This portion of the prayer may be used as a litany, with the congregation praying the words that are printed in italic.

9. A major hurricane had just struck the shore of North Carolina and left in its wake an unprecedented flood in most of the eastern part of the state. The First Presbyterian Church of New Bern, North Carolina, for whom this prayer was written, had risen powerfully to the occasion and was providing flood relief in the form of goods, home repairs, and stability. Simultaneously, the news of the day was filled with stories about devastating earthquakes.

10. This portion of the prayer may be used as a litany, with the congregation praying the words that are printed in italic.

11. This prayer was written during the time when the election between Al Gore and George W. Bush had not yet been settled.

12. This portion of the prayer may be used as a litany, with the congregation praying the words that are printed in italic.

CHAPTER 4: PRAYERS FOR OTHER TIMES
THE EXILES ARE GATHERED FOR WORSHIP

1. This portion of the prayer may be used as a litany, with the congregation praying the words that are printed in italic.

2. This portion of the prayer may be used as a litany, with the congregation praying the words that are printed in italic.

3. This portion of the prayer may be used as a litany, with the congregation praying the words that are printed in italic.

4. John 1:5.

5. Adapted from Isaiah 60:1.

6. Jayne Lowry and Darren Stanhouse were married on May 5, 2001.

7. A solo cello provided service music for worship.

8. Margaret Lowry and Brian Brock were married on July 10, 1999.

9. I wrote this prayer in the form presented here for the funeral of my mother-in-law, Leila Lewis Nichols (August 5, 1905–May 30, 2000). The Rev. Tony Medlin, then pastor of the Mount Dearborn United Methodist Church in Great Falls, South Carolina, used the prayer in her funeral service. She died full of years and great wisdom. I used versions of the prayer previously and have used versions of it since.

10. The prayer may be easily adapted by fitting the italicized words and phrases to the occasion.

11. Alfred G. Smith (July 17, 1935–May 5, 2001) was the father of my colleague Shirley Smith Rogers. Shirley and I worked together at the First Presbyterian Church in New Bern, North Carolina. Al and Thelma Smith reared their only daughter on a farm near the town of Pikeville in the mountains of East Tennessee. I was unable to be present for worship at her father's funeral but sent this prayer to be used at the service.

12. The prayer may be easily adapted by fitting the italicized words and phrases to the occasion.

13. Walk C. Jones III (July 4, 1933–August 13, 1998) was an elder in the Idlewild Presbyterian Church in Memphis, an architect by profession, and a member of many boards and agencies. Notably, he was a member of the board of Louisville Presbyterian Theological Seminary. This prayer was written for graveside worship with only family present. Public worship was held at the Idlewild Church following the graveside service. On the edge of retirement, he died of an aggressive malignant brain tumor.

14. Gary Taylor (August 24, 1954–December 27, 1992), a member of the Idlewild Presbyterian Church in Memphis, was shot down in his front yard. The gunman followed him from an automatic teller machine where he had gone to get cash to pay a baby-sitter. He was survived by his wife, Kathy, a daughter, Alison, and a stepson, Blake.

15. Mary Elizabeth Calhoun (July 2, 1912–March 1, 1998) was a member of the Idlewild Presbyterian Church in Memphis. Having cared for her invalid husband for many years, she died suddenly and unexpectedly.

16. Virtually all pastors are faced from time to time with the awkward circumstance of being asked to conduct funeral worship for a person the pastor has never known. This prayer is for such an occasion.

17. The following is a service of lessons and prayers conducted on the night of September 11, 2001, the date on which four jetliners were hijacked by terrorists and crashed: two into the twin towers of the World Trade Center in New York City, one into the Pentagon outside Washington, D.C., and the fourth falling short of its target into a field near Pittsburgh. The service, conducted with the congregation of the Government Street Presbyterian Church in Mobile, Alabama, proceeded with the lessons as noted being read. Each reading was followed by a brief time of silence and then the prayers as noted were offered.

18. This prayer was written for the newly appointed search committee for an academic dean at Columbia Theological Seminary in Decatur, Georgia. D. Cameron Murchison was the answer to this prayer.

19. Working under funding provided by a grant from the John Bulow Campbell Endowment, the Campbell Scholars are an international group of theologians and pastors brought together annually for eight weeks by Columbia Theological Seminary of Decatur, Georgia. The task of the seminar is to discuss the mission of the church as the church moves into the twenty-first century. Walter Brueggemann, William Marcellus McPheeters Professor of Old Testament at Columbia, moderated the 2000 seminar. Other members were Joanna Adams, (then) pastor of Trinity Presbyterian Church in Atlanta; Russel Botman, professor of theology and missiology, University of Stellenbosch, South Africa; Douglas John Hall, emeritus professor of Christian theology, McGill University, Montreal, Canada; James S. Lowry, (then) interim pastor of First Presbyterian Church, New Bern, North Carolina; Damayanthi Niles, (then) of the Christianity in Asia Project, faculty of divinity, St. John's College, University of Cambridge, England; Ofelia Ortega, president of the Protestant Theological Seminary, Matanzas, Cuba; and Janos Pasztor, former dean of the Reformed Theological Seminary in Budapest, missionary to Kenya, and pastor in Hungary. The findings of the 2000 Campbell Seminar were published by Westminster John Knox Press in 2001 under the title *Hope for the World: Mission in a Global Context.*

20. The litany, to this point, was taken from the headlines of the morning paper.

21. The Campbell Scholars agreed early on that *despair* is the theological construct out of which the church must work as it moves into the twenty-first century.

22. Billie Slater is a faithful member of the First Presbyterian Church of New Bern, North Carolina. During the time I was interim pastor there, she was involved in a serious automobile accident. Mercifully, for long months after the accident she had no memory of either the accident or its immediate aftermath. She did, however, remember in finest detail her dreams during those first nights after the accident and delighted in telling me about them . As I was leaving her hospital room following a pastoral visit, she asked me to write a poem for her. This prayer is the answer to her request. We were the only two exiles gathered when it was offered. There is no medical evidence that she died and was revived during her ordeal.

CHAPTER 5: PRAYERS OF EXILES PRAYING OUTSIDE THE CAMP

1. Each year on April 4, the anniversary of the assassination of Dr. Martin Luther King Jr., a prayer vigil is held in Memphis on the balcony of the Loraine Motel, the site where the famous civil rights leader was gunned down in 1968. On several of those occasions I was asked to offer prayers on behalf of the hundreds gathered in the parking lot below the balcony. This is one of those prayers.

2. The Memphis Interfaith Association is a large social service agency. It was formed by the Jewish and Christian communities in response to overwhelming needs in the city that came

into focus following the assassination of Dr. Martin Luther King Jr. This prayer is one of many I offered at the monthly meetings of its board of directors.

3. Each year, the Memphis chapter of the National Association for the Advancement of Colored People holds a gala banquet at the famous Peabody Hotel in Memphis. The gala never fails to be a grand and festive event. The year in which this prayer was offered, Vice President Al Gore was the keynote speaker.

4. William Gibbons is the district attorney general for Shelby County, Tennessee. This prayer was written for and delivered at the ceremony in which he was sworn into office.

5. Relay for Life is a national fund-raising network that sponsors local marathon relays to raise funds for cancer research. This prayer was delivered in a carnival atmosphere in an athletic stadium.